SAINT JOHN CHRYSOSTOM

Six Books on the Priesthood

SAINT JOHN CHRYSOSTOM

Six Books on the Priesthood

Translated
with an Introduction
by
GRAHAM NEVILLE

ST VLADIMIR'S SEMINARY PRESS
CRESTWOOD, NY 10707
1996

Library of Congress Cataloging-in-Publication Data

John Chrysostom, Saint, d. 407
   [De sacerdotio. English]
   Six books on the priesthood / John Chrysostom; translated, with an
introduction by Graham Neville.
        p.   cm.
   "This translation is a thoroughly revised version of T. A. Moxon's
translation, published by S.P.C.K. in 1907"—Pref.
   Originally published: London: S.P.C.K., 1964.
   ISBN 0-913836-38-9 (alk. paper)
   1. Clergy—Office. I. Title.
BV4011.J63   1996
262'.14—dc20   96-31820
                                                                  CIP

First printed in 1964 by S.P.C.K.

This edition first printed 1977 by
ST VLADIMIR'S SEMINARY PRESS
1-800-204-2665

Reprinted 1984, 1996

ISBN 0-913836-38-9

PRINTED IN THE UNITED STATES OF AMERICA

CONTENTS

PREFACE

IN PRESENTING a new version of St John Chrysostom's Six
Books on the Priesthood to English readers of the twentieth
century, I should like to make four brief explanatory com-
ments. They concern the form in which the work is
presented, the translation used, the meaning of "the priesthood", and the reason for reading Chrysostom's work to-day.

First, then, the form of the present edition does not follow
the customary division into six books; the text has been
divided instead into sixteen chapters. The reason is that the
present edition is intended primarily for reading and not for
reference, and the traditional division corresponds only
partially with the natural division of the work by subject-
matter. The scope and development of the work can be
better appreciated by a rearrangement into chapters. For
those who wish to refer to the original text, each page of
this book carries a marginal reference, by book and section,
to the Greek text as printed in Migne's *Patrologia Graeca*,
volume 48.

The translation is a thoroughly revised version of T. A.
Moxon's translation, published by S.P.C.K. in 1907. Both
that translation and this revision are based upon the critical
text of J. A. Nairn, published in the series *Cambridge
Patristic Texts* in 1906. In revising Moxon's translation I
have had four objects in view : the correction of a small
number of errors, the elucidation of St John Chrysostom's
meaning where Moxon left it ambiguous, the elimination of
many archaic phrases, and the tautening of Moxon's rather
diffuse style.

The work is entitled *Concerning the Priesthood—*

περὶ ἱερωσύνης. But in fact Chrysostom was really concerned specifically with the episcopate. He does not normally refer to bishops (ἐπίσκοποι) but to priests (ἱερεῖς). But the content of the Six Books makes it quite evident that he had a bishop's work in mind, and it was to the episcopate that his friend Basil was forcibly consecrated *per saltum*, as it was a similar consecration that John evaded. But no thoughtful observer of the present-day ministry and no student of the patristic Church will need to be told that there is no exact correspondence between the division of functions among the orders of ministry to-day and the division which was customary in the eastern Church of the fourth century. Much, therefore, which the reader will find here *à propos* the episcopal order can be applied with little variation to the parish priest of to-day.

In saying that, I have given already some reason for reading the Six Books to-day. To be more specific, the priest, and indeed the layman, will find much that is helpful and suggestive, as well as much that warns of dangers, in the discursive thoughts of so warm and human, so intelligent and spiritual an observer of the Church as John Chrysostom. The case for reading this work is incidentally argued in the following Introduction. It rests fundamentally on the fact that, whatever the differences of age and nation, the ministry is always and everywhere the same ministry of Word and Sacraments, and has always and everywhere the same challenge and hope—to bring men and women to Christ, that he may do his own strange work in their lives. Let us agree or disagree with this or that statement of Chrysostom; we are learning still, by agreement or disagreement, to see more clearly the glory and the hazards of the priesthood.

G.N.

INTRODUCTION

OF THE three best known patristic writings on the Priesthood, each has its distinctive character. The qualities of John Chrysostom's treatise *On the Priesthood* are best appreciated, and its defects best understood, by comparison with the other two.

The first in order of writing and the shortest of the three is Gregory Nazianzen's apologetic composition, usually referred to by its Latin title, *De Fuga*. In spite of being reckoned among Gregory's "Orations", it is, like Chrysostom's work and Pope Gregory's *Book of Pastoral Rule*, a literary work, elaborating a brief apologetic discourse which he delivered at Nazianzus at Eastertide in A.D. 362. The circumstances which gave rise to the original discourse and its elaboration were that Gregory's father, the Bishop of Nazianzus, had ordained him, much against his will, to the priesthood at the preceding Christmas. Immediately after his forcible ordination, Gregory abandoned his father's church and returned to the solitude of Pontus, where till then he had been pursuing the Christian "philosophy" of a monk's life. On mature consideration he regretted this precipitate abandonment of what he came to believe had been (however strangely ministered) a divine call to the priesthood. His chilly reception by the church people of Nazianzus induced him to explain and defend his action—and to give to later Christian generations the meditations of a sensitive and subtle mind on the responsibility and the privilege of such a divine vocation.

He begins by brushing aside any suggestion that he had shirked the office and work of a priest through ambition for

9

other, more worldly, distinctions—a suggestion which Chrysostom, too, felt the need to refute, and at greater length. He then lists four reasons for his withdrawal: the sheer shock of his forcible ordination, his long-standing love of retirement from the world, his shame at those who intruded without qualifications into the ministry ("as if they thought this order to be a means of livelihood instead of a pattern of virtue, or an absolute authority instead of a ministry of which we must give account"), and finally his belief that he was unqualified for a position in which it would be all too easy to infect those set under him.

Gregory then illustrates the difficulty of a priest's work by comparing it with that of a doctor. The priest's is the harder task because he deals with souls that resist their own healing instead of bodies that co-operate; because spiritual disease is hidden, whereas physical ailments are apparent; and because he aims, not simply to preserve or restore health, but to "deify those who belong to the heavenly host". Nothing less than this was the purpose of the Incarnation. Where doctors work merely to extend a possibly sinful life, we (says Gregory) work for the salvation of the soul. And because we deal with many different types of men, we must continually vary our methods, not only according to their differences, but also as times and circumstances change. It is as tricky a job as tight-rope walking!

Then there is the ministry of the Word. With the comprehension of a subtle theologian, Gregory dilates upon the problem (all too real in his day) of communicating orthodox Trinitarian doctrine to a mixed and largely uneducated congregation, their minds full of preconceived ideas, or self-conceit, or plain ignorance, or the kind of muddle-headedness which leads through confusion to general scepticism.

The problem is not simply to teach them the truth, but to disabuse their minds of false doctrines.

We may well ask, Who is sufficient for such a problematical task? It is better to go on learning than to try teaching without the assurance of one's own ability. It is altogether too perilous to try "teaching practice" and learn by your own mistakes (Gregory says, "Learn the potter's art on the wine-jar"). There is far too much pretended learning in the Church already. Only a Peter or a Paul could handle the situation.

At this point Gregory calls on the aid of the Scriptures, first to witness to the astonishing life and character of St Paul (and so to point the contrast of his own incapacity), and then to provide a whole catena of texts drawn from the Old Testament prophets, all on the theme of judgement, the particular and relentless judgement in store for the leaders of God's people when they betray their incomparable trust. It is enough to make a man tremble for his own salvation, let alone the responsibility of ruling others. Would it not be better, says Gregory, at least to wait? A priest is not made in a day. "Who can mould, as clay-figures are modelled in a single day, the defender of the truth, who is to take his stand with angels, and give glory with archangels, and cause the sacrifice to ascend to the altar on high, and share the Priesthood of Christ, and renew the creature, and set forth the image, and create inhabitants for the world above, aye, and, greatest of all, be God and make others God?"

Deeply moved by the sacred duties of the priesthood, conscious that it has been given to him to understand something of the mystery and majesty of God, and responsive to the vocation which his very home and upbringing seem to urge upon him, Gregory is half won to the acceptance of his

unsought ministry. But his attention turns from the ideal of
the priesthood to the harsh realities, not of the world, but
of the Church. How can he take on himself the guidance of
others in such troubled times—the Church profaned, invec-
tive prized, personal rivalries flourishing, all in chaos and
confusion? Priests and influential laymen are involved in
the strife. Pagans hate us for our dissensions. Our own best
people are scandalized. The Christian is even lampooned on
the stage. His own disciples make Christ's name to be
blasphemed.

In these circumstances the probability of failure is great.
Gregory hesitates again. He recalls the stringent demands of
the Scriptures for purity alike in priest and sacrifice. He
thinks of the punishment of Nadab and Abihu, of Eli, and
of Uzzah. "How could I dare", he asks, "to offer to God
the external sacrifice, the antitype of the great mysteries, or
clothe myself with the garb and name of priest, before my
hands had been consecrated by holy works; before my eyes
had been accustomed to gaze safely on created things, with
wonder only for the Creator, and without injury to the
creature; before my ear had been sufficiently opened to the
instruction of the Lord, and he had opened my ear to hear
without heaviness, and had set a golden ear-ring with
precious sardius, that is, a wise man's word in an obedient
ear; before my mouth had been opened to draw in the
spirit, and opened wide to be filled with the spirit of speaking
mysteries and doctrines; and my lips bound, to use the words
of wisdom, by divine knowledge, and, as I would add,
loosed in due season; before my tongue had been filled with
exultation, and become an instrument of divine melody,
awaking with glory, awaking right early, and labouring till
it cleave to my jaws; before my feet had been set upon
the rock, made like hart's feet, and my footsteps directed in a

godly fashion so that they should not well-nigh slip, nor slip at all; before all my members had become instruments of righteousness, and all mortality had been put off, and swallowed up of life, and had yielded to the Spirit?"

With such an exalted view of the spiritual qualities and the preparation needed for the work of the priestly ministry, Gregory's natural inclination had been to refuse ordination. He had no opinion at all of those who, though not yet able to take up the Cross, eagerly accepted the priesthood. And when ordination had been thrust upon him, his impulse had been to escape, back to his chosen solitude. And as he writes his apologia, he recalls how he used to say : Let others run great risks; I prefer to plough a short but pleasant furrow.

But in the end his fears and his preferences give way to what he cannot avoid regarding as his duty. His affection for the people of Nazianzus and theirs for him combine with his respect for his parents to draw him back to his own town, his own people, and the responsibilities of the priestly office. Even Jonah may have had his excuses, says Gregory, but not I. It is true that a man is only worthy of the sanctuary after he has shown himself worthy of the Church, and only worthy of the presidency after he has shown himself worthy of the sanctuary. But though the fear of inadequacy is strong, the fear of disobedience is stronger, because of the grave penalties attached to it. There is no excuse for the disobedient; at least there is the promise of grace for the weak. I withdrew to consider. I have returned to serve. Here am I, my father; bless me. May God hold me by my right hand and guide me with his counsel.

There could be nothing more serious-minded in its appraisal of the priestly office than this; and nothing more attractively ingenuous than the self-examination of a man at once wise in learning and simple in faith. Throughout the oration the writer holds our sympathy. And in this, as we shall see, he is more successful than John Chrysostom. That is one difference between the two men and their compositions on the priesthood. Another lies in the contrasted styles in which they write. Gregory's style, though not without the tricks of oratory, gives an impression of artlessness. His sentences are seldom involved in structure. He achieves the weight and effectiveness of his words largely by parataxis, by the accumulation of parallel clauses. Chrysostom, on the other hand, has a style branded with the imprint of the schools of rhetoric. His sentences are often elaborately constructed, far more syntactical than Gregory's, and loaded with internal contrasts and verbal duplication. Seventeenth-century England might have conferred on him the title of "John of the Golden Mouth", but not twentieth-century England, fed on a diet of journalism, in which a subordinate clause is almost a monstrosity and certainly a mistake. Even by less jejune standards than these, *On the Priesthood* may well appear to us to-day stylistically lush, as a good deal of Chrysostom's writing may seem emotionally florid. We ought, perhaps, to put some of this down to his Antiochene temperament. But the shadow of that pagan orator, Libanius (if indeed he were, as is probable, Chrysostom's teacher), lies across the treatise on the priesthood.

It falls across his style, it may be traced in the form into which the book is cast and the ingenuity of the defence of deceit which it contains, and it is visible in the speech which Chrysostom puts into the mouth of his mother in Book I of the treatise. No doubt opinions must vary on the effectiveness of this speech. The greatest living authority on John Chrysostom, Dom Chrysostomus Baur, says of it:

"This entire passage . . . belongs among the finest and most delicate pearls of ancient Christian literature".[1] Other readers with more emotional self-consciousness might sum it up with the rude epithet "tear-jerking". But on either assessment it bears the marks of that training in composition which Chrysostom received in the pagan schools; and if the result be accounted a defect in taste, it is one from which Gregory of Nazianzus, for all his training in similar schools, is happily free.

There are other differences between Gregory's oration and Chrysostom's dialogue which call for no judgement of comparative value. For they do no more than illustrate the saying of St Paul, that there are diversities of gifts, but the same spirit. The words of Gregory, as has been hinted, are the words of one who cannot help being a theologian, and a speculative theologian at that. Even his reflections on his call to the priesthood lead him into the niceties of the doctrine of the Holy Trinity. Chrysostom imitates Gregory in a short discursus on Trinitarian theology, but he is a fundamentally different kind of person.

He was above all a moralist rather than a speculative theologian, and none the worse for that. The Antioch and the Constantinople of his priesthood and his episcopate had surely had their fill of speculative theology, with all the bitterness it brews when compounded with ecclesiastical power-politics. In the providence of God, Chrysostom came to the sacred ministry after the accession of Theodosius had given a measure of theological peace to the Church. It was a time for the preaching of plain Christian morality. And that was Chrysostom's great gift—the gift that made his

---

[1] *John Chrysostom and his Time* (E.T.), Vol. I, p. 106. Cf. W. R. W. Stephens, *Saint Chrysostom* (1872), p. 27, "a dramatic power worthy of Greek tragedy".

reputation and afterwards occasioned his exile and premature death.

His enduring title, "of the Golden Mouth", might suggest "a very lovely song of one that hath a pleasant voice and can play well upon an instrument"; it might imply the ability to pour forth a stream of "beautiful truths", as they are called, a flow of spiritual consolations from one whose feet hardly seem to touch the solid, work-a-day earth. Nothing could be further from a true description of John Chrysostom and the gift that has given him a name among the great. He had a mind both practical and idealistic, that brought into close connection the evils and injustices of the world and the perfection of moral life demanded by the Gospel. That was the source of his power as a preacher, as it was also the cause of his sufferings as a Patriarch. In his treatise on the priesthood he moves easily, and without doubt or any sense of constraint, within the limits of theological orthodoxy, applying his mind principally to the practical aspects of that sacred ministry.

Both Gregory and Chrysostom, as befits their theme, turn to the Scriptures of the Old and New Testament to establish and to illustrate their teaching, and it is here that one other difference between the two men becomes apparent. Gregory shows himself to be one of the "Cappadocian Fathers"; Chrysostom, a follower of the Antiochene school of exegesis. Gregory treats scripture as possessing, in addition to its plain literal meaning, another, spiritual, meaning of equal or even greater importance. This kind of interpretation, arising from a Platonic view of the material order as being a shadow or reflection of eternal reality, is not largely obtruded in the particular work under consideration. Gregory almost launches on a spiritual interpretation of the story of Jonah, towards the end of his oration; but he realizes it would be out of place, and promises to elaborate it in a separate writing. Otherwise there are only slight indications of his tendency to spiritual exegesis. They are, however, just enough to remind us of the greater restraint of that method of interpretation which Chrysostom had learnt at Antioch from Diodore, in which the whole weight was thrown upon the literal, historical meaning of the text, and other kinds of meaning were looked for only when the text would otherwise remain unintelligible or unedifying. In this the modern age prefers Antioch to Cappadocia. If there is anything in Chrysostom's exegetical method which grates on a modern ear, it is his refusal to admit any ignorance in our Lord's human nature. In the dialogue on the priesthood there are one or two examples which show how this refusal makes Chrysostom treat the questions which Jesus put to others as having some purpose other than to get information. This, on Chrysostom's presuppositions, he could not need, since he was omniscient.

At this point, having drawn from the contrast with Gregory of Nazianzus some illustrations of the qualities of Chrysostom's treatise, we may turn to another contrast, afforded by Pope Gregory the Great in his *Book of Pastoral Rule*. For in Pope Gregory's book the thing which is most likely to deter a modern reader is his method of scriptural exegesis. What are we to make of a passage like this? "It is well said to Ezekiel, The priests shall not shave their heads, nor suffer their locks to grow long, but polling let them poll their heads. For they are rightly called priests who are set over the people for affording them sacred guidance. But the hairs outside the head are thoughts in the mind; which, as they spring up insensibly above the brain, denote the cares of the present life, which, owing to negligent perception, since they sometimes come forth unseasonably, advance, as it were, without our feeling them. Since, then, all who are over others ought indeed to have external anxieties, and yet should not be vehemently bent upon them, the priests are rightly forbidden either to shave their heads or to let their hair grow long; that so they may neither cut off from themselves entirely thoughts of the flesh for the life of those who are under them, nor again allow them to grow too much." The final conclusion is unexceptionable. But it has nothing to do with Ezekiel 44.20; and we can be sure that Chrysostom would not have supposed that it had.

The *Book of Pastoral Rule* is much less like the *De Fuga* and Chrysostom's dialogue on the priesthood than they are like each other. It is cast in the form of a systematic treatise with four parts. The subjects of the four parts are : the qualifications for rule; the life of the ruler; the teaching of the ruler; and the ruler's need for self-criticism. The four parts are of very different size, the fourth being only a brief peroration, and the great bulk of the book falling into part three. The method Gregory adopts here is to describe in a series of thirty-six admonitions the different ways in which the bishop should deal with the many different types of people in the Church. This method was apparently suggested by a hint in the *De Fuga* (written some two hundred years earlier), since Pope Gregory mentions its author in the prologue to this part of his book; though he cannot have known Gregory Nazianzen's writing in the original, for he knew no language but Latin. The different types of people are treated in contrasted pairs—e.g. the forward and the fainthearted, the impatient and the patient. The book, therefore, is an exercise in contrasts, for not only does Gregory take antithetical pairs of types, but, as is illustrated by the curiosity of exegesis quoted above, he tends to arrive at his conclusions by setting the limits within which action

18

must fall. His theme is, indeed, "not too little, not too much"; the ruler must be severe to sin, but not too severe; he must be gentle with the weak, but not too gentle, and so forth. There is, without question, much that is of the greatest value here for the curate of souls. But, as F. D. Maurice observed in *The Conscience*, if such general rules are thought to remove the need for personal advice, they fail in their purpose, since doubts about their application are bound to arise, and can be resolved only by personal advice.[2] In fact, the form of the book, though helpful to writer and reader for the marshalling of material, is likely to be misleading, because its systematic arrangement suggests the provision of ready-made answers to pastoral problems. No such answers exist. Moreover, the greatest variable factor in Pastoral Rule—the character of the Ruler—is omitted from consideration.

It does not follow, therefore, that Chrysostom's less systematic approach is necessarily a hamper to the usefulness of his treatise. If he is handicapped by anything, it is by the strange discussion of deceit with which the greater part of Book I is taken up. Most readers must surely find themselves all too soon out of sympathy with Chrysostom when they begin to read a book on the priesthood, and find that they have to plough their way through an unsatisfying, casuistical argument, to the effect that we may sometimes deceive even our friends for a good purpose (the end justifying the means). But the argument must be expounded, and right at the beginning of the work, because of the real or imaginary circumstances which gave rise to it. And here we touch on one point which the three patristic writings under discussion

[2] F. D. Maurice, *The Conscience*, Lecture V: Rules of the Conscience.

have in common : they all take their origins in their authors' unwillingness to accept ecclesiastical office.

The circumstances in which Gregory of Nazianzus wrote the *De Fuga* have already been noticed. His namesake was leading the life of a monk in a monastery of his own founding at Rome, when Pope Pelagius II died in A.D. 590. He was elected to fill the vacant dignity, but attempted to prevent the confirmation of his election by the Emperor. In this he was unsuccessful. He is also said to have escaped in disguise and hidden in a cave, where a pillar of light miraculously disclosed his presence to his pursuers. We may think that there is more substance underlying the story than the mere convention of "Nolo episcopari". For the monastic life had its rewards as well as its disciplines, and the times were not happy for any occupant of the Papal see. At any rate, the consideration of his own reluctance and the gravity of the spiritual office entrusted to him was the occasion of his writing the *Book of Pastoral Rule*.

The truth about the origin of John Chrysostom's work on the priesthood is perhaps less certain. If we take Book I at its face value, we must suppose that he and a friend called Basil (possibly the Basil who attended the Council of Constantinople in A.D. 381 as Bishop of Raphanea) had been marked out for consecration to the episcopate while still laymen and still below the canonical age for ordination to the priesthood, which the Council of Neocaesarea had fixed at thirty. John heard in advance what was intended and went into hiding, with more success than the future Pope Gregory. Basil suspected nothing, and was subjected to forcible consecration. The dialogue *On the Priesthood* purports to record what passed between John, the layman, and Basil, the bishop, when they met again after these events. It is, of course, a written-up account; no one supposes it to be a literal transcript of the interview. But did any such meeting ever take place?

Those who admire John Chrysostom most will be predisposed to accept the view that the setting of the dialogue is entirely fictitious,[3] because if it is really true, it shows John in a discreditable light. But there is no escape from this discredit. Suppose the setting to be never so imaginary, the defence of these imaginary actions is still there, and John is the author of them. We cannot acquit him of the charge of dangerous casuistry (in the worst sense) in his defence of deceit, whether fictitious or real. And, as if that were not bad enough, there is an intolerable smugness in his attitude to his perplexed friend. We could forgive his actions, if he showed a trace of shame, or even of doubt about their propriety. Our sympathy might not be alienated if he remained impenitent but showed some compunction for his friend's sake. But none of these conditions is fulfilled. He is wide open to criticism, whether or not the assumed circumstances of the dialogue had any historical reality.

But still the question remains : did it happen to Basil and John as the dialogue says it did? The earliest biographer of John Chrysostom (in *Dialogue of Palladius*) makes no mention of any early attempt to ordain him.

He was gifted with unusual ability, and was carefully trained in letters, for the ministry of the oracles of God. At the age of eighteen, a boy in years, he revolted against the professors of verbosities; and a man in intellect, he delighted in divine learning. At that time the blessed Meletius the Confessor, an Armenian by race, was ruling the Church of Antioch; he noticed the bright lad, and was so much attracted by the beauty of his character, that he

[3] See D. Attwater, *St John Chrysostom, Pastor and Preacher* (1959), p. 27.

allowed him to be continually in his company. His prophetic eye foresaw the boy's future. He was admitted to the mystery of the washing of regeneration, and after three years of attendance on the Bishop, advanced to be reader. But as his conscience would not allow him to be satisfied with work in the city, for youth was hot within him, though his mind was sound, he turned to the neighbouring mountains; here he fell in with an old man named Syrus, living in self-discipline, whose hard life he resolved to share. With him he spent four years, battling with the rocks of pleasure. [His austerities led to the breakdown of his health and] as he could not doctor himself, he returned to the haven of the Church. . . . Next, after serving the altar for five years, he was ordained deacon by Meletius.[4]

Here is the normal pattern of progress to ordination, and no mention of the threat of forcible and uncanonical preferment. But the silence of the author of the *Dialogue of Palladius* is really no evidence either way. For he must have known John's work *On the Priesthood*, and, as he does not use it as historical evidence, so also he does not contradict it explicitly. It seems, therefore, that he shared the uncertainty with which we too are forced to remain content. We can only say that an attempted uncanonical ordination was no unlikely thing, since other cases are well attested, and that if it was simply part of a fictitious setting for the dialogue, John was guilty of a considerable lapse of taste, to say the least, in representing himself as having been selected for a dignity which in fact he had never been offered.

Equal uncertainty attaches to the date of John's composition. It has been argued[5] that it was written shortly after his

[4] *The Dialogue of Palladius*, trs. H. Moore (1921), pp. 37–9.
[5] ΠΕΡΙ ΙΕΡΩΣΥΝΗΣ *of St John Chrysostom*, ed. J. A. Nairn (1906), pp. xii–xiii.

ordination to the priesthood in A.D. 386, since a sermon of his, which cannot have been preached before that date, promises that he will treat of the priesthood and its dignity "on another occasion". But this may be no more than the promise of a sermon on the priesthood, which there would certainly be nothing to prevent John preaching long after the publication of a book on the same subject. And the various ecclesiastical writers of the following centuries who mention the composition, though they do not all give the same date, at least agree in assigning it to a period before A.D. 386.

There is a small point bearing on this question which does not seem so far to have been noticed. In Book III (10–11) Chrysostom argues that the holder of ecclesiastical office (in this context he means a bishopric) should not wait to be deposed, but should voluntarily retire, if he commits a sin worthy of deposition. Otherwise he adds a second, more serious, offence to that which he has already committed. But, continues Chrysostom, "no one will ever be content to do so".[6] Now it is well known that in A.D. 381 Gregory of Nazianzus did in fact voluntarily resign the see of Constantinople, and although it was not for the sake of past sins but future peace that he did so, it is difficult to believe that a few years later Chrysostom would have written the words quoted above.

All things considered, it is best to accept Book I as providing a substantially true account of John Chrysotom's early life, early call to the sacred ministry, and rejection of that first call. We can then suppose, quite naturally, that during his time of retirement in the desert (before A.D. 381)

---

[6] ἀλλ᾽ οὐδεὶς ἀνέξεταί ποτε. T. A. Moxon (Early Church Classics series, 1907, p. 74) wrongly translates: "No one will always endure the strain." The Greek cannot bear this meaning.

he elaborated his apologia for having refused ordination. In doing so, he may have turned to the *De Fuga* of Gregory Nazianzen, with which his own dialogue shows points of similarity.[7] If so—and there can be little doubt that he had read the earlier work—it may be no coincidence that Chrysostom repeated at a more leisurely pace the change of mind which, as we have seen, led Gregory back to Nazianzus and the work of the sacred ministry. Was it perhaps the composition of the dialogue on the priesthood which itself worked this conversion? The last Book (VI) ends with two far-fetched similes designed to illustrate the absurdity of making John a bishop. We are asked to compare the idea of consecrating him to episcopal rule with marrying a lovely young girl to a hideous and perverted man, or putting a magnificent army under the command of a simple shepherd boy. Hearing these comparisons, Basil, who has not been allowed to speak for a good many pages, suddenly comes alive again and says, in effect, "But what about me?" And John has no proper answer. He has overreached himself and proved that virtually no one is fit for the sacred ministry. It is a true, but hardly a useful, conclusion. John finds only one thing left to say : that the help of Christ is available for those who undertake this ministry. In so doing, he repeats the conclusion of the *De Fuga*, and exposes himself to the retort : "Is not that grace available for you too?" We know that it was, in full measure. It seems to have taken John a good six years to learn to trust that grace.

The Six Books on the Priesthood form a somewhat shapeless entity, although Chrysostom has made some effort to treat of the various aspects of his subject in order. Book I is entirely taken up with the real or fictitious events which called it forth : John's friendship with Basil and the

[7] See Nairn, op. cit., p. xxx.

bitterness caused by what Basil considered his betrayal into a bishopric. Book II continues the personal argument with Basil, though it contains (pp. 54–9) some general observations on the nature of the priestly office, arising from an exploration of the simile of a shepherd and his sheep. At first it looks as if Chrysostom is taking this simile too literally, for he says that there ought to be a difference of spiritual stature between priest and people even greater than that between the human shepherd and the dumb animals he has charge of. But fortunately he abandons this line of thought once it has served his purpose of explaining his own sense of unworthiness. It may be all right as an antidote to the misapplication of the truth contained in Article XXVI : that the unworthiness of the minister does not hinder the effect of the sacrament. But the Church never has been served by a ministry of such gigantic spiritual stature; and though the priest can never aim too high in spirituality, the idea that he is to be a different kind of being from the layman can only mislead priest and layman alike, and destroy the unity of the Church. Chrysostom must have been aware of this. For in the development of his comparison between priest and shepherd he emphasizes, not their likeness, but their difference. The shepherd may compel his flock to submit to the treatment which he knows to be for its good; the priest must win the co-operation of his people for their spiritual good, and must take into account the difference in character between one man and the next. This, as we have seen, was the main burden of Pope Gregory's *Book of Pastoral Rule*. But Chrysostom, no more than Gregory, reckons with the differences in character of individual pastors.

In Book III Chrysostom all but completes his personal apologia for refusing office. The theme recurs from time to time, and appears as a formal conclusion of Book VI, to pull the whole work together. But much of the middle section of the work has little reference to the original issue, and Basil almost disappears from the dialogue, being allotted no more than the occasional interjection as his (very unepiscopal) contribution to it.

The substance of Book III can be analysed into three parts: (a) §§ 4-10. General remarks on the priesthood, its power and its dangers; (b) §§ 10-14. General remarks on the qualities required in a bishop; (c) §§ 15-18. Particular duties and difficulties. The first part is characterized by comparisons of the priest and the king, and the priest and the father. Such comparisons look as though they owe their origins to the secular schools of rhetoric at which Chrysostom was educated. The way they are developed shows a preoccupation with power which marked and marred Chrysostom's character to the end; for he argues that the priest's power is greater than the king's power over his subjects or the father's over his children. He is right when he stresses the incomparable benefits which the faithful priest may confer through his ministry. But he is misled by his own comparisons into speaking as though the priest had authority over his own ministry of absolution, and could by his own choice withhold forgiveness. For his absolution is the declaration with authority of that relation with God in which the penitent already stands by virtue of his penitence. The priest does not by absolution create that relation, nor can he negate it by failing or refusing to absolve. The only bar to forgiveness lies in the impenitent heart of the sinner. It must follow, therefore, that the function of the absolving priest is to convey authoritatively the assurance of a relationship with God which already exists because of mercy offered and accepted. It is a dangerous half-truth to interpret

Matthew 18.18 and John 20.23 as meaning that whatever the priest does on earth, God confirms or ratifies[8] above. The initiative is with God, not man. No priest can force or restrain God's hand. The comparison of priest and king is false, because the king acts by sovereign right, the priest by commission.

In the same context there is a similar confusion of thought about the priest's power over Baptism and the Eucharist. The priest has no self-inherent power to celebrate or not to celebrate the Eucharist or to administer or withhold Baptism. In both sacraments he acts for Christ in his Church. Freedom of choice, therefore, lies only with Christ in his Church, and not with the priest as distinct from the Church (a concept which is basically nonsensical), let alone with the priest apart from Christ. In short, here as in the question of absolution there can be no comparison of priest and king. The only valid comparisons would be those of God and a king, or of a priest and an executive officer. And even then there would be lurking dangers. For the Church has all the uniqueness of the unique Incarnation which is both its source and its sustaining life. Its functional differentiation into various orders within the one ministry may be illustrated, but cannot be explained, by comparison with other organisms and organizations.

The particular qualities which Chrysostom selects as prerequisites for ecclesiastical office (§§ 10–14) called for little comment. The apologia theme is still being worked out, and so the qualities mentioned are rather those which he feels he lacks, than those most important for the exercise of the ministry in question. He mentions in particular freedom from ambition, the ability to carry in his head and on his heart the affairs of many people, and the full mastery of his

[8] P. 72. Chrysostom's words are κυροῖ καὶ . . . βεβαιοῖ.

own temper. In each of these he adjudges himself deficient.

The remainder of Book III is occupied with certain practical problems. First comes the question of ensuring the preferment of the right men in the Church. We are given a picture of promotion by democratic, not to say demagogic, methods beside which the barest nepotism seems no very terrible thing. Chrysostom then points out that the care of widows is far from being a matter of merely financial administration. It requires, he says, in the administrator unusual gifts of patience and tolerance, because widows are notoriously voluble and querulous! The relief of the sick is another exacting duty, and for much the same reason. The care of virgins, too, is a heavy responsibility, made even more difficult by the fact that the priest must not know them too familiarly, for his own sake and theirs, and yet must watch over them even more carefully than a father over his unmarried daughters. But although Chrysostom touches on these practical matters, he does not aim to give practical advice. They are just illustrations of his theme: the difficulty and responsibility of the priest's work. There is nothing to show that, when he wrote, he had any closer acquaintance with the problems he mentions than that of an intelligent and perceptive member of a Christian congregation.

Books IV and V are about preaching. And that is interesting, partly because it reveals the man (and possibly the layman) who wrote this work, and partly because it shows that the fourth century had more in common with the nineteenth than the twentieth. If we recall that the first two Books are chiefly concerned with the argument between Basil and Chrysostom about the circumstances in which one was ordained and the other evaded ordination, we must reckon that about a third[9] of the space devoted to the discussion of the priesthood is given to the topic of preaching. It reveals the man who was first trained in secular oratory, who was to make his name at Antioch as a preacher, and who made his enemies and brought about his own downfall at Constantinople to a large extent by his preaching. In his struggle with Theophilus, Patriarch of Alexandria, he met a man who has left no great name as a preacher, but an unenviable reputation as an intriguer. And you cannot defeat intrigue by preaching. After his recall from his first brief exile, he finally alienated the Empress Eudoxia by a sermon which was a deliberate, public challenge to her. We cannot but admire Chrysostom's refusal to meet the intriguer with his own weapons, and his indifference to the dangers of challenging a worldly Empress. But in historical retrospect we can see that his actions, right as they were, and inevitable for a man of his particular character, led by short steps to schism in the Church of Constantinople, the subjugation of the ecclesiastical to the civil power, and the beginning of the decline of the second see of Christendom. The whole history of the Eastern Church might have been very different if the greatest of Constantinople's Patriarchs had shown a little more of the wisdom of the serpent. It might even have been different if he had possessed a more moderate genius for preaching, or trusted and valued less his supreme gift.

The fault, however, was the fault of the age. Even England in the nineteenth century, with its cult of preaching and the published sermon, could not have outdone Antioch and Constantinople in the fourth century. In those two great metropolitical sees people thronged to hear the preachers, applauded or studiously refrained from applauding—and

[9] Books IV and V together are only about as long as Book III.

went out of church before the Holy Mysteries were offered. It was no less (and sometimes no more) than a public entertainment. And so there are two Books out of six on the preaching office.

It is unlikely that any priest to-day would devote a third of his working time to the preparation and delivery of his sermons, though it was not uncommon in the last century.[10] Indeed it would be labour misapplied, now that Church congregations imagine themselves incapable of attending for more than fifteen minutes on end. Yet it is probably still true, at least in the towns, that "the majority of church-goers judge a minister by the way in which he treats one particular part of his duties—the delivery of a sermon".[11] And even if this is only half true, it is still profitable for the present-day priest to consider the thoughts about preaching which occupied Chrysostom's mind in the days before his greatness as a preacher. He will not find in what Chrysostom has to say any instruction in the technique of preaching. He would not find it any more in the treatises of the two Gregories. For the common education of the ancient world, which lacked so much that we expect of education to-day, was largely concerned with one thing which we neither find nor expect to-day : training in the arts of public speaking. Chrysostom, therefore, could take the technique for granted (even if its description had been germane to his theme, which it was not). He is free to discuss the qualities required in the preacher. It is true that he includes among them the ability to speak forcefully, which was a prime necessity in a sermon-tasting age. But there are no hints about its cultivation. It is mentioned as something without which other good qualities may produce no effect, since nothing is easier

[10] See E. D. Mackerness, *The Heeded Voice* (1959), p. xv note 1.
[11] Mackerness, op. cit., p. xi.

than to forget a man's meaning in the process of criticizing his style.

The two great qualities which Chrysostom saw to be needed in the preacher were indifference to praise or blame and a grasp of theological orthodoxy. The one is a moral and the other primarily an intellectual gift. It might be argued that neither is as important now as then. For on the one hand our congregations are more reticent about their appreciation or dislike of particular sermons, and on the other hand interest in the niceties of theology among laymen seems to have reached its nadir, now that so many Christians of all kinds have adopted the slogan, "We are all going the same way". But this is a superficial view. We may not need the same kind of theological acumen in our preachers, and lay criticism or appreciation may not be expressed in such audible or unmistakable ways. But moral independence and intellectual perception are no less required now than then. It is still true that the preacher feels the pressure of criticism and the inducement to conform. He still must avoid the twin temptations of preaching to please and ignoring just criticism because he has become content with his own mediocrity as a preacher. If the latter is only hinted at in Chrysostom's treatise, it is because he knew already that it was not likely to be his own temptation. The other needed gift, of theological acumen, must take new shape in every age. In the age of the great heresies and the great doctrinal Councils, when, as Chrysostom testified,[12] few were keenly interested in the practical bearing of faith on life and every man thought himself a theologian, fit to define the hidden things of God, no doubt the preacher needed to be able to steer his way carefully between the hidden rocks on either side of orthodoxy in Trinitarian and Incarnational theology.

[12] p. 119.

In our own age the climate of thought is far different. And though it remains necessary rightly to believe the Trinity and Incarnation, something more is required. The Christian's voyage is through seas uncharted by the definitions of ecumenical councils. His pilot must discover a channel between the perils of popularized science, materialistic social philosophies, half-understood psychology, and plain selfishness disguised as a noble protest against the "establishment". It is quite an assignment for the preacher of fifteen-minute sermons.

But the value of Books IV and V will be lost if we confine their relevance to preaching. In fact, Chrysostom's subject is teaching, as his own words make clear. In the multitudinous congregation of Antioch the principal method had to be by the set sermon. To-day the technique must be different. The short sermon has become the vehicle for conveying one or two simple ideas. In the majority of parishes that limitation must be accepted. But because the Christian faith has more to it than a few simple ideas, there must be something else beside short sermons. There must be adult education. For, as Chrysostom says,[13] in dealing with spiritual ailments we have only one technique and method of healing, beside the example of a good life, and that is teaching by word of mouth. "This is the best instrument, diet, and climate. This serves us instead of medicine, cautery, and surgery." Each age must develop its own methods, and we have no right to expect an ancient Father to provide us with a blue-print for the modern world. But the basic fact remains, that there must be good teaching, if the priest is to promote the spiritual health of the congregation. Words are his weapons and he must know how to use them.

In the last Book (VI) Chrysostom returns from the

[13] p. 115.

consideration of the teaching ministry to some more general observations about the qualities required in a bishop. Much of it is taken up with another of those comparisons of which he was so fond; in this case the comparison of the bishop and the monk. We may see here the statement of convictions which he had reached by inner debate during his own period as a solitary. Some of his first literary productions had been written in defence of the monastic life. Their apologetic purpose had inclined him to minimize the possible criticisms of such a life. But now the practical bent of his character had brought him to realize its limitations. The moralist in him wanted to change and reform the corrupt society of his day. If he continues to refuse ordination, it is not because he thinks the monastic life superior, but because he does not feel himself fit for the supreme task of the sacred ministry; at least, not yet.

He had taken two steps towards ordination. The first was the rejection of worldly ambition, of which the sign was his writing of the *Comparison of a King and a Monk*. The second was the recognition of the supremacy of the pastoral ministry, of which the sign was this other comparison of a monk and a bishop, in the treatise on the priesthood. The difference between the two comparisons is instructive. The first is governed by the concept of power : the monk's life is better, because he exercises a superior kind of power to the king's. The second is governed by the concept of practical usefulness : the monk's life unfits him for the supreme responsibility of the pastoral ministry. As an interesting aside to his main theme in the second comparison, Chrysostom observes that the monastic life is dependent on favourable circumstances (good bodily health, a suitable climate, arrangements to allow him to be self-supporting); whereas the bishop can do his work anywhere and in all circumstances. But his real theme is the supremacy of the pastoral ministry and the exacting demands it makes upon those who exercise it. And this theme leads back to the point of departure of the whole treatise—Chrysostom's refusal of ordination for no other reason than his sense of unworthiness.

It is fascinating to watch the process of his vocation to the sacred ministry. First we picture the intelligent, attractive, rich young man, with a good career at his feet. Then comes the renunciation of that career, but not the renunciation of the most alluring of its gifts : power over others. The monastic life is regarded as a means to even greater power, as though every monk was a kind of "éminence grise". The next stage is the renunciation of this pcwer and its replacement by the desire to be among men "as he that serveth". The fulfilment of this desire is blocked only by fear—fear of his own failure and the punishment it would bring. There we leave Chrysostom at the end of the treatise *On the Priesthood*. Beyond that point must have come the enabling word : "My grace is sufficient for thee."

We cannot, of course, take Chrysostom's vocation and generalize from it. But any ordinand might well look within himself for some analogue of its movement. So might any priest, however mature in his ministry. For Chrysostom did not complete his renunciations till the day of his death. Much less do we.

Saint John Chrysostom
SIX BOOKS ON THE PRIESTHOOD

1

JOHN'S DECEIT

I USED to have many genuine and true friends, who knew the laws of friendship and observed them strictly. But there was one in this group who outstripped them all in his friendship for me and set his heart on leaving the rest as far behind him as they did the people who regarded me with indifference. He was one of my constant companions. We went in for the same studies and attended the same teachers. We had an equal eagerness and enthusiasm for the studies at which we were working, and the same high ideals produced by common interests. Not only while we were at school, but when we left it and had to decide what career would be best to choose, we were clearly of one mind. And besides all this, there were other bonds which held unbroken and secure. Neither of us could boast more than the other of his country's greatness. Nor had I too much money while he lived in extreme poverty; on the contrary, our means were as matched as our views. Our families were of the same class and everything was in keeping with our common opinions.

But when the time came to enter upon the blessed life of the monks and the true philosophy, the balance no longer remained even. His scale rose lightly upwards, while I, still fettered with worldly desires, dragged my scale down, weighting it with youthful vanities, and forced it to stay on a lower plane. From that time our friendship remained firm as before, but our intimacy was broken. For we could not share our activities when our interests diverged.

But when I, too, emerged slightly from the surge of life,

he received me with open arms. Yet not even then could we maintain our former equality; for he had got the start of me, and by displaying intense earnestness, was rising far over my head and was reaching great eminence. Still, since he was such a good man and valued my friendship highly, he withdrew from all the rest of his friends, and spent his whole time with me. He had been anxious to do this before, but, as I explained, he had been hindered by my indifference. For it was impossible for anyone who was always at the law-courts, and was thrilled by the pleasures of the stage, to associate often with a man who was glued to his books and never even went out into the market-place. For this reason he was cut off from me. But as soon as ever he had got me to follow the same plan of life as himself, he quickly pro-duced the scheme which he had conceived long before. He would not leave me alone for a moment, but persisted in advocating that we should each abandon his own home and share a place together. He succeeded in persuading me, and the arrangements were in hand.

But the unceasing entreaties of my mother prevented me from doing him this favour—or rather, from accepting it from him. As soon as she saw that this was my intention, she took my hand and led me to her own private room. Sitting close by me on the bed on which she had given me birth, she burst into tears, and then spoke words more touching than tears. And this was her sad complaint :

"My child," she said, "I was not for long permitted to enjoy your father's virtues, for so it pleased God. His death followed very soon after my travail over you, and left you an orphan and me a widow before my time, with all the burdens of widowhood, which only those who have borne them can properly understand. No words could describe the stormy sea which a young girl faces, if she has only just left her father's house without any experience of the world, and is suddenly struck with unbearable sorrow and compelled to shoulder cares too great for her age and sex. For, as I know too well, she has to correct the carelessness of servants, to guard against their misconduct, to thwart the schemes of relatives, and to bear with dignity the insults of public officials and their rudeness about payments of tax. And if her dead husband should have left a child, even when that child is a girl she will cause great anxiety to her mother, though not expense and fear. But a son fills her with a host of misgivings every day that passes, and even more anxieties. I say nothing of the heavy expenditure she must incur if she wants to bring him up as a gentleman. Still, none of these thoughts persuaded me to contract a second marriage and to introduce another husband to your father's house. No, I remained patient, while troubles surged around me, and I did not flinch from the iron furnace of widowhood. My chief help was from above. And I found great consolation in those trials in gazing continually at your face and treasuring in you a living and exact image of my dead husband. So while you were still a baby and had not even learnt to speak, at the time when children give most pleasure to their parents, you afforded me great comfort. You cannot even make it a reproach against me that I bore my widowhood with dignity, but only at the price of reducing your patrimony, through a widow's necessity—a fate which, I know, a good many who have had the misfortune to be fatherless have suffered. No indeed; I kept it all intact—and I did not omit any expenditure which your reputation demanded, but paid it from my own purse and from the dowry which I brought from my home.

"Please do not think I am telling you this now as a reproach to you. But in return for all this I ask for just one favour : not to inflict on me a second bereavement and rouse again my sleeping grief. Be patient till my death. It may be I shall depart before long. Those who are young look forward to a distant old age; but we who have grown old have nothing to wait for but death. When you have committed me to the ground and united me with your father's bones, then set out on your long travels and sail whatever sea you please. Then there will be nobody to hinder you. But until I breathe my last, be content to live with me. Do not give needless offence to God by overwhelming me with such misfortunes, for I have never done you any harm.

"Of course, if you have reason to complain that I distract you with worldly cares and make you manage my property, then pay no attention to nature's laws or education or custom or anything else, but shun them as traitors and enemies. But if, on the contrary, I do everything to provide you with plenty of leisure for the pursuit of this kind of life, then let this bond, if nothing else, keep you by my side. Even if you argue that you have a thousand friends, not one will let you enjoy such freedom as this, for there is nobody who cares for your reputation as I do."

All this and more my mother said to me, and I repeated to that good friend of mine. But, so far from being put out by these arguments, he was all the more insistent in his original requests.

While we were in this position—he constantly entreating and I not giving way—suddenly a rumour reached us which threw us both into confusion. The rumour was that we were to be promoted to the dignity of the priesthood. For my part, as soon as I heard this story, I was overcome with fear and bewilderment : with fear, that I should be seized against my will, and with bewilderment, as I tried again and again to guess what had induced the men concerned to form such a

plan for me. I examined myself and could discover nothing
that deserved such an honour.

That good friend of mine came to me privately and shared
the news with me, thinking I had not heard the rumour, and
begged that in this too, as in other things before, we might
be seen to act and to decide together. He said that he was
ready to follow my lead in either course, whether to escape
or let ourselves be taken. However, I knew his keenness, and
I reckoned I should be to blame in the eyes of the whole
congregation of the Church, if through my own weakness I
should deprive the flock of Christ of a young man so good
and so well fitted to govern. So I did not let him see what I
thought about this, although I had never before dared to
hide any of my opinions from him. But I said we ought to
put off considering the question to another occasion, as at
present it was not urgent, and persuaded him not to worry
about it just then. I made him feel confident in me, that I
should act in concert with him, if by any chance this kind
of thing should happen.

But when a short time had passed, and the one who was
to ordain us had come, I remained in hiding, while he, knowing nothing of this, was taken off on some other pretext.
He submitted to the yoke, expecting from my promises to
him that I too should certainly follow, or rather, thinking
that he was following me. For some of the people with him,
when they saw he was restless about being captured, deceived him by calling out that it was strange that the one
everybody considered the more head-strong (meaning me)
had bowed to the decision of the fathers with full submission,
while the one who was far more reasonable and submissive
acted so boldly and conceitedly, leaping about and shying
off and arguing the point.

At this he gave way. But when he heard that I had

escaped, he came to me in great dejection and sat by my side. Then he tried to speak, but was prevented by his indignation. He just could not give his words the force he was waiting to summon up. No sooner did he open his mouth than speech failed him, for despondency cut his words short before ever they passed his lips. So when I saw he was choked with tears and full of distress, knowing the cause, I began to laugh for sheer delight, and taking his hand I made him embrace me. And I glorified God because my stratagem had turned out well, as I had always prayed it might. But when he saw that I was so pleased and cheerful and realized that he had been taken in by me, he was all the more wounded and disconsolate.

2

BASIL'S REPROACHES

WHEN AT last he had calmed down a little from his agitation of mind, he said :

Even if you have washed your hands of me and respect me no longer (though I do not know why), you should at least have considered your own reputation. As it is, you have set every tongue wagging. Everyone is saying that it was through the love of worldly honours that you declined this ministry. And there is no one to clear you of this imputation. Personally, I cannot bear even to go to the market-place, so many there are who come up to me and reproach me every day. Whenever they see me in daylight anywhere in the city all my intimate acquaintances take me aside and impute the greater share of the blame to me. "Since you knew his intentions", they say, "—and none of his plans was ever hidden from you—you ought not to have concealed them. You should have passed them on to us. You may be sure we should not have been at a loss for some trick in the hunt." And I am covered with shame. I blush to tell them that I did not know you had been planning this for a long time, for fear they should think our friendship a mere sham. If in fact it is—and surely it must be, and you cannot deny it yourself after what you have just done to me—it is only right to hide our troubles at least from strangers and from those who have an indifferent opinion of us. So I shrink from telling them the truth and the real state of affairs be-tween us, and I am constantly compelled to hold my peace and stare at the ground and avoid people who meet me and bolt off. For if I clear myself of the charge I have mentioned,

I shall inevitably be thought a liar, as they will never bring themselves to believe that you treated Basil no better than all the others who have no right to know your secrets.

But this is no great matter to me, since you are so pleased with what has happened. But how shall I bear the shame of their other accusations? Some accuse you of arrogance and others of worldly ambition, and the more brutal of these accusers level both charges equally against us and for good measure add the accusation of insolence towards those who did us an honour. They say it would have served them right if they had been treated even more contemptuously by us, since they passed over men of quality and experience, and took mere striplings who only yesterday or perhaps the day before got engrossed in the cares of the world (or seemed to, if for a moment they screwed up their faces and put on sub-fusc and assumed a pensive look!), and suddenly exalted them to greater dignity than they had ever dreamed of attaining. Men who from their earliest years to a ripe old age have maintained their self-discipline are under authority, and their rulers are their children who have never so much as heard of the laws which ought to guide them in exercising their authority.

They dog my footsteps unceasingly with these reproaches and more of the same sort. And I do not know what answer to make to them. I beg you to tell me. For I suppose it was not without due thought and reflection that you made your escape and so incurred the serious hostility of such important people. You must have reached this decision after careful reckoning and inquiry. And so I infer that you have some reason ready to give in your defence. Tell me, then, whether I shall be able to offer any good excuse to those who accuse you. I do not demand any satisfaction for the wrong you have done to me or for your deceit or your treachery or for

the favours you have enjoyed from me in the past. I brought
my very soul and, so to speak, placed it in your hands. But
you have used as much craft towards me as if your concern
was to guard against an enemy. And yet, if you knew their
plan was good, you should not have refused the advantage
yourself; and if you thought it harmful, you should have
saved me too from the loss, since you always professed to
think more of me than of others. But you actually did everything to make me fall into the trap, and you resorted to
trickery and pretence in dealing with the very one who in
word and act towards you was always open and sincere.

But still, as I said before, I bring no such charge against
you now; nor do I reproach you with the wilderness into
which you have led me by bringing to an end those times
together which often gave us unusual pleasure and profit.
I pass over all that. I accept it, humbly and silently—not
because your offence against me showed any humility, but
because I have made it a rule for myself, since the day I first
formed my friendship with you, that I would never demand
an explanation of any pain you might choose to cause me.
To be sure, you know yourself that you have inflicted on me
no little punishment—unless you have forgotten what was
said about us repeatedly by strangers, and by ourselves, to
the effect that it was a great advantage for us to be united
and secure in our mutual friendship. Everyone else said our
concord would be a great help to a lot of other people. I,
personally, never thought about its helping anyone else; but
I did say we should get at least one great advantage from
it, that we should not be easy victims to people who wanted
to get the better of us.

I never stopped reminding you of this. "The times are
dangerous," I said. "Our enemies are many. True love is
dead. The poison of malice has taken its place. We 'go

about in the midst of snares and walk upon battlements of cities'.[1] There are many all round us who stand ready to rejoice over any misfortune that might happen to us. There are few, if any, to share our sorrow. Take care we do not incur a lot of ridicule, and penalties worse than ridicule, if we are ever divided. 'A brother by a brother helped is as a strong city and a kingdom securely barred.'[2] Do not part this true love; do not cut through this secure bar."

All that and more I was for ever saying, though I never suspected anything like this. On the contrary, I thought your disposition towards me was sound and that I was wanting gratuitously to heal the healthy. But it seems I was unwittingly administering medicine to a sick man. And even so I, poor fool, did not effect my purpose; nor have I got any reward from my excessive forethought. You discarded my advice all at once and laid none of it to heart. You have turned me adrift like a vessel without ballast on a boundless ocean and given no thought to those cruel waves with which I must contend. When I happen to meet with calumny or mockery or any other kind of insolence or abuse (and that kind of thing must often occur), to whom shall I run for help? To whom shall I confide my fears? Who will agree to help me? Who will check those who trouble me and make them stop, and comfort me and equip me to endure the ill-mannered conduct of others? There is no one, if you stand aloof from this dreadful warfare and cannot even hear the din of battle. Do you know how much harm you have done? Do you realize, even now after striking me, how deadly is the blow you have dealt?

But let it pass. We cannot undo what is done or find help for the helpless. But what shall I say to the world at large? What reply shall I make to their charges?

[1] Ecclus. 9.13.   [2] Cf. Prov. 18.19 (LXX).

3

JOHN'S REPLY

JOHN : Take courage ! I am not only ready to let myself be questioned about this, but I will also try to explain, as far as I can, those other matters you have excused me from explaining. And, if you like, I will make them the very opening of my defence. For I should be unnatural and quite unfeeling, if I were anxious for the good opinion of strangers and exerted myself to prevent them from accusing us, and yet should fail to acquit myself in the eyes of my greatest friend; and that although he has treated me with such gentleness that he will not accuse me for my supposed injuries to him, but sets his own interests aside and can still think of mine. It would be strange if I seemed more casual about him than he is concerned about me.

How, then, did I wrong you? For this is where I have decided to embark upon my defence. Is it that I misled you and concealed my own intention? But this was for the advantage both of yourself who were deceived and of those to whom I betrayed you by my deception.

For if fraud is always wrong and we cannot use it when we need, then I am ready to pay any penalty you like. Or rather, as you will never consent to bring me to court, I will pronounce the verdict against myself, as jurors do against criminals when they are convicted by their accusers. But if it is not always harmful; if it is made bad or good by the intentions of those who use it, stop accusing me of deception, and prove that I used this means for an evil end. For while this proof is lacking, it remains the duty of those who want

47

to be fair, so far from finding fault and criticizing, rather to give their approval to the deceiver. A timely deception used with a right purpose is such an advantage that a lot of men have been called to account on many occasions for failing to deceive.

If you consider famous generals from the beginning of history, you will find that most of their successes are triumphs of deceit, and that men like this can earn more praise than others who conquer by straightforward methods. For the others are successful in their wars at a greater expense of money and men; and so they gain no advantage from their victory, but the victors suffer almost as much as the vanquished, both in loss of life and in financial loss. Moreover their methods do not allow them to enjoy the whole credit of the victory. For even the fallen enjoy no small part of it, because they were victorious in spirit and vanquished only in body, so that, if they had been able not to fall when hit, and if death had not come to stop them, they would never have halted in their eagerness. But the man who can conquer by deceit involves his enemy not only in disaster but also in ridicule. It is not a case of both sides carrying off equal honours for shrewdness—as in the other instance for valour. No, the prize belongs to the victors alone. What is more, they keep for their country the joy of victory unimpaired. For shrewdness of mind is not like wealth in money or man-power. When you use them continually in war, the supply becomes exhausted and fails its possessors. But the more you use shrewdness, the more it will increase.

Not only in war, but in peace too, you can find many cases in which the use of deceit is necessary, and not only in public life, but in domestic matters. A husband needs it for a wife, a wife for a husband, a father for a son, a friend for a friend, and sometimes even children for a father. Saul's daughter could not have rescued her own husband by any other device from her father's grasp except by tricking him. And when her brother wanted to save from danger the very man she had rescued, he, too, used the same weapons as she did.

Basil: None of this applies to me. I am not a foe or enemy or one who plans to hurt you, but just the opposite. I always entrusted all my plans to your decision, and used to follow the path you told me to take.

John: Why, my dear good friend, this is the very reason why I got my word in first and said that it is right to use deceit, not in war only, nor only with enemies, but in peace and with our best friends.

To discover how useful deceit is, not only to the deceivers but to the deceived, go to any doctor and inquire how they cure their patients of diseases. You will hear them say that they do not rely on their skill alone, but sometimes they resort to deceit, and with a tincture of its help they restore the sick man to health. When the plans of doctors are hindered by the whims of their patients and the obstinacy of the complaint itself, then it is necessary to put on the mask of deception, in order to conceal the truth about what is happening—as they do on the stage.

With your permission, I will relate to you one of the many tricks which, I have heard, doctors devise. Once a fever fell suddenly upon a patient very violently, and his temperature kept rising. The sick man refused the medicine which would have allayed the fever, but longed and insisted, with requests to everyone who visited him, that he should be given a long drink of neat wine and be allowed to take his fill of the deadly thing he wanted. It would not only have inflamed the fever but have thrown the poor man into a hemiplegia, if anyone had granted him this favour. In this case, where professional skill was baffled and at the end of its resources and quite useless, deception stepped in and showed the extent of its power, as you shall now hear.

The doctor took an earthenware vessel fresh from the kiln and steeped it in wine. Then he took it out empty and filled it with water. Next he gave orders for the room where the patient was lying to be darkened with thick curtains, for fear that the daylight might show up the trick. He then gave the vessel to the patient to drink from, pretending it was full of neat wine. The patient was deceived, even before he took it into his hand, by the aroma that reached him. He did not stop to examine closely what was offered to him. Convinced by the aroma, deceived by the darkness, and impelled by his craving, he snatched the vessel impatiently. And when he had drunk his fill, he immediately shook off the fever and escaped his imminent danger.

Do you see the advantage of deception? If you were to collect all the tricks of doctors, the list would stretch interminably. And you will find that it is not only those who heal the body who constantly use this remedy, but those who treat the diseases of the soul, too. By this means St Paul won over all those thousands of Jews.[1] With this intention he circumcised Timothy,[2] even though he wrote to the Galatians that Christ would not profit those who were circumcised.[3] On this account he became subject to the Law[4]—he who reckoned the righteousness of the Law but loss after finding faith in Christ.[5]

Great is the power of deceit; only it must not be applied with a treacherous intention. Or rather, it is not right to call such action deceit, but good management and tact and skill enough to find many ways through an impasse, and to cor-

---

[1] Acts 21.20.   [2] Acts 16.3.   [3] Gal. 5.2.
[4] 1 Cor. 9.20.   [5] Phil. 3.7.

rect the faults of the spirit. I should not call Phinehas a murderer, though he took two lives with one blow,[6] nor Elijah, in spite of the hundred soldiers and their captains [7] and the great river of blood he made flow from the slaughter of those who sacrificed to devils.[8] If we were to allow that description, a man could strip all action of the intention of the agents, examine it out of context, and, if he liked, condemn Abraham for murdering his son,[9] and accuse his grandson and his descendant of evil-doing and fraud, since it was by this means that the one gained the privileges of the first-born,[10] and the other transferred the wealth of the Egyptians to the host of the Israelites.[11]

But this will not do, it will not do! Perish the presumption! We not only acquit them of blame, we revere them for these very things, since God praised them on their account. He alone can justly be called a deceiver who performs the action for unjust ends, since it is often necessary to deceive and by this means aid great causes. The straightforward man does great harm to those he will not deceive.

[6] Num. 25.7–8.   [7] 2 Kings 1.10, 12.   [8] 1 Kings 18.40.
[9] Gen. 22.10.   [10] Gen. 27.   [11] Ex. 11.2.

4

THE DIFFICULTY OF PASTORAL CARE

I COULD have argued at greater length that it is possible to use the power of deception for a good end, or rather that it is not right to call that kind of action deceit at all but an admirable kind of good management. But since I have said enough to prove my case, it would only be wearisome and tedious to prolong my argument. Now it is up to you to show that I have not used this method to your advantage.

Basil: What kind of advantage have I got from this good management or wisdom or whatever you please to call it, to persuade me that I was not deceived by you?

John: Why, what greater advantage could there be, than to be obviously doing what Christ himself declared was proof of love for Christ? Speaking to the chief of the apostles, he said, "Peter, lovest thou me?"; and when Peter confessed that he did, he added, "If thou lovest me, tend my sheep." The Master asked the disciple if he loved him, not to learn the truth—why should he, who lives in all men's hearts?—but to teach us how much he cares for the supervision of these flocks. Once this is evident, it will be equally obvious that a great, indescribable reward will be in store for the man who works hard at the tasks which Christ values so highly. When we see anyone caring for our slaves or our flocks we take his concern for them as a sign of his love for us—although they can all be bought for money. What gift, then, will he give as a reward to those who shepherd his flock, which he purchased, not for money or any such thing, but by his own death when he gave his blood for his flock's ransom. And so when the disciple said, "Thou knowest, Lord, that I love thee", and called as a witness of his love the one he loved, the Saviour did not stop there but went on to describe the proof of love. He did not want to prove then how much Peter loved him (which was already clear to us from many pieces of evidence), but he wanted Peter and all of us to learn how much he loves his own Church, in order that we too might show great concern for the same thing.

Why did God not spare his only-begotten Son but surrendered the only Son he had? It was to reconcile to himself those who hated him and to make them a people of his own possession.[1] Why did he shed his blood? It was to purchase the sheep which he entrusted to Peter and his successors. Those words of Christ, then, were natural and fair: "Who is the faithful and wise servant whom his Lord shall set over his household?"[2] Again the words denote perplexity but their speaker was not perplexed when he spoke them. On the contrary, as when he asked Peter if he loved him, he did not ask because he wanted to know his disciple's affection, but because he wanted to show his own exceeding love; so also when he asked the question, "Who then is the faithful and wise servant?", he did not ask this because he did not know the faithful and wise man, but because he wanted to show how few there are and how important is this office. Notice, at any rate, the magnitude of the reward: "He will set him over all that he hath."[3]

Will you continue, then, to dispute with me that you were well deceived, if you are going to be set over all God's possessions, and are doing what the Lord said Peter would be able to outstrip the rest of the disciples by doing? For he said, "Lovest thou me, Peter, more than these? Tend my sheep." He might have said to him, "If thou lovest me,

[1] Titus 2.14.   [2] Matt. 24.45.   [3] Matt. 24.47.

practise fasting, sleeping on the bare ground, and prolonged vigils; champion the wronged; be 'as a father to the fatherless and instead of a husband to their mother'.[4] In fact, he passes over all this. And what does he say? "Tend my sheep."

The other things I have mentioned could easily be carried out by many of those under authority, women as well as men. But when someone has to preside over the Church and be entrusted with the care of so many souls, then let all womankind give way before the magnitude of the task—and indeed most men. Bring before us those who far excel all others and are as much above the rest in spiritual stature as Saul was above the whole nation of the Hebrews in bodily stature—or rather, far more. Let us not look for a difference only "from the shoulder and upward"[5] but let the difference between shepherd and sheep be as great as the distinction between rational and irrational creatures, not to say even more, since matters of much greater moment are at stake.

A man who loses sheep through the ravages of wolves or the attacks of robbers or through murrain or some other accident, might perhaps meet with a measure of pardon from the owner of the flock. Even if he is called upon to pay compensation, the penalty stops at money. But anyone entrusted with men, the rational flock of Christ, risks a penalty not of money but of his own soul for the loss of the sheep. Moreover, he has a far greater and more difficult struggle. His fight is not with wolves; his fear is not of robbers; his care is not to protect the flock from pestilence. Well then, against whom is the war? With whom is the battle? Listen to St Paul. He says, "Our wrestling is not against flesh and blood, but against the principalities, against powers, against

[4] Ecclus. 4.10.　　　[5] 1 Sam. 9.2.

54

the world rulers of this darkness, against the spiritual hosts of wickedness in the heavenly places."[6] Do you see the terrible host of enemies and the savage legions, not armed with steel, but relying on their own evil nature instead of any armour?

And would you like to be shown another cruel and savage army, which is lying in wait for this flock? You can see this, too, from the same point of vantage. The same man who spoke about the others shows us these enemies as well, speaking somewhere like this: "Now the works of the flesh are manifest, which are these: fornication, adultery, uncleanness, lasciviousness, idolatry, sorcery, enmities, strifes, jealousies, wraths, factions, backbitings, whisperings, swellings, tumults,"[7] and more besides these. For he did not list them all, but let us recognize the rest from these examples.

In the case of the shepherd of irrational creatures, those who want to destroy the flock stop fighting with him when they see him running away, and are content to seize his animals. But in the other case, even if they snatch the whole flock, they do not leave the shepherd alone, but attack him all the more, act with more daring, and do not give up until they either throw him down or are beaten themselves. Besides this, the sufferings of animals are obvious—starvation, pestilence, injury, or anything else that might harm them. This is a great help in ridding them of their troubles.

And there is something else more important than this which makes the cure of this kind of disease rapid. What is it? Shepherds have full power to compel the sheep to accept the treatment if they do not submit of their own accord. It is easy to bind them when it is necessary to use cautery or the knife, and to keep them shut up for a long time when that is the right thing, and to introduce different kinds of food

[6] Eph. 6.12.   [7] Cf. Gal. 5.19–21 and 2 Cor. 12.20.

one after another, and to keep them away from water. And all other remedies the shepherds think will promote the animals' health they apply with perfect ease.

But human diseases in the first place are not easy for a man to see; for "no one knows the things of a man save the spirit of the man which is in him".[8] How, then, can anyone provide the specific for a disease if he does not know its character and often cannot tell whether the man is ill at all? When it becomes apparent, then it is all the more intractable to him. You cannot treat men with the same authority with which the shepherd treats a sheep. Here too it is possible to bind and to forbid food and to apply cautery and the knife, but the decision to receive treatment does not lie with the man who administers the medicine but actually with the patient. That wonderful man, Paul, knew this fact when he said to the Corinthians, "Not that we have lordship over your faith, but are helpers of your joy."[9] For Christians above all men are forbidden to correct the stumblings of sinners by force. When secular judges convict wrong-doers under the law, they show that their authority is complete and compel men, whether they will or no, to submit to their methods. But in the case we are considering it is necessary to make a man better not by force but by persuasion. We neither have authority granted us by law to restrain sinners, nor, if it were, should we know how to use it, since God gives the crown to those who are kept from evil, not by force, but by choice.

For this reason a lot of tact is needed, so that the sick may be persuaded of their own accord to submit to the treatment of the priests, and not only that, but be grateful to them for their cure. If a man struggles when he is bound (for he may

[8] Cf. 1 Cor. 2.11.   [9] 2 Cor. 1.24.

56

still choose to do so), he makes his sufferings worse. And if he ignores the words which cut like steel, he adds a second wound through his contempt, and the intention to heal becomes the occasion of a more serious disease. For the man does not exist who can by compulsion cure someone else against his will.

What, then, should you do? If you behave too leniently to one who needs deep surgery, and do not make a deep incision in one who requires it, you mutilate yet miss the cancer. But if you make the needed incision without mercy, often the patient, in despair at his sufferings, throws all aside at once, medicine and bandage alike, and promptly throws himself over a cliff, "breaking the yoke and bursting the bond".[10] I could tell you of many who have been stranded in utter misery because they were called to pay the full price of their sins.

It is not right simply to exact a penalty by the measure of the sins; some guess must be made about the disposition of the sinners, for fear that when you want to stitch up what is torn, you should make the tear worse, and in your eagerness to help up the fallen you should cause a worse fall. Those who are weak and dissipated and generally in bondage to worldly luxury—even more if they can pride themselves on their birth and rank—may be freed partially, if not perfectly, from the evils which master them, by being converted gently and gradually from the sins they commit. But if anyone applies a sudden restraint, he deprives them even of this small improvement. For once a soul is forced to be brazen, it becomes callous and thereafter neither responds to gentle words nor is checked by threats nor is influenced by kindness, but becomes much worse than the city which the

---

[10] Cf. Jer. 5.5.

prophet reviled, saying, "Thou hadst a whore's forehead; thou refusedst to be ashamed before all." [11]

So the shepherd needs great wisdom and a thousand eyes, to examine the soul's condition from every angle. As there are plenty of people who are puffed up into arrogance and then fall into heedlessness of their own salvation because they cannot stand bitter medicines; so there are others who, because they do not pay a proportionate penalty for their sins, are misled into negligence and become far worse, and are led on to commit greater sins. The priest, therefore, must not overlook any of these considerations, but examine them all with care and apply all his remedies appropriately, for fear his care should be in vain.

The shepherd of sheep has the flock following him wherever he leads; or if some turn aside from the direct path and leave the good pasture to graze in barren and precipitous places, it is enough for him to call more loudly, drive them back again, and restore to the flock those which were separated. But if a man wanders away from the right faith, the shepherd needs a lot of concentration, perseverance, and patience. He cannot drag by force or constrain by fear, but must by persuasion lead him back to the true beginning from which he has fallen away. He needs, therefore, a heroic spirit, not to grow despondent or neglect the salvation of the wanderers, but to keep on thinking and saying : "Peradventure God may give them the knowledge of the truth and they may be freed from the snare of the devil." [12]

That is why the Lord, speaking to the disciples, said : "Who, then, is the faithful and wise servant?" The man who practises asceticism helps no one but himself. But the advantage of a shepherd's skill extends to the whole people.

[11] Jer. 3.3.   [12] Cf. 2 Tim. 2.25–6.

The man who distributes alms to the needy or in other ways defends the wronged, has done some good to his neighbours; but less than the priest, as the body is less than the soul. It is not surprising, then, that the Lord said concern for his sheep was a sign of love for himself.

5

LOVE—THE CHIEF THING

BASIL : But you—do you not love Christ?

John: Yes, I love him and shall never stop loving him. But I am afraid of provoking the one I love.

Basil: Could any paradox be more obscure? Christ commanded the man who loved him to tend his sheep, and you say that your reason for not tending them is that you love the one who gave this command !

John: What I said is no paradox, but a clear and simple statement. If I had been qualified to administer this office as Christ wished, and then had refused it, you might well have been puzzled by what I said. But since the infirmity of my spirit makes me useless for this ministry, what have I said that is open to criticism? I am afraid that if I receive the flock from Christ plump and well-fed and then damage it through ineptitude I may provoke against me God who so loved it that he gave himself for its salvation and redemption.

Basil: You are not talking seriously. For if you were, I do not know how else you could have proved the justice of my resentment more clearly than by the argument with which you mean to dispel my despondency. I knew already that you had deceived and betrayed me, but now that you are trying to refute my charges, I understand and realize all the more fully what a plight you have landed me in. If you extricated yourself from such an office because you knew that your spirit was unequal to the responsibility of the work, you should have rescued me from it first, even if I had been full of eagerness for it—quite apart from the fact that I entrusted to you the entire decision about our actions. As it is, you regarded yourself and forgot me. Or rather, I only wish you had forgotten me! Then I should have been content. But you plotted to make me an easy prey to those who wanted to get hold of me.

You cannot even take refuge in the plea that popular opinion deceived you and led you to suspect great and marvellous things of me. For I am not one of your famous and distinguished men. And even if I had been, you ought not to have preferred popular opinion to the truth. If I had never let you enjoy my company, you might have seemed to have a reasonable excuse for giving your verdict in accordance with common report. But since no one knows me as well as you; since you know my inner nature better than my parents who brought me up : what argument can you find strong enough to convince those who hear it that you did not deliberately push me into this danger?

However, let that pass now. I will not insist that you answer these charges. But, tell me, what reply shall we make to those who criticize us?

John: No, I will not pass on to that until first I have made it up with you, however willing you may be to release me from answering these charges.

You said that ignorance would have condoned my offence and freed me from all responsibility, if I had known nothing of your character, and so had led you on to your present position; but that since I betrayed you in spite of not being ignorant but knowing your character quite well, all just excuse or reasonable defence was precluded. But I maintain the opposite. And why? Because questions like this need close examination. If someone is about to present another man as fit for the priestly office, he must not be content merely with popular report, but in addition to this he ought, beyond and before all else, to examine that man's character himself.

For when St Paul said, "Moreover he must have good testimony from them that are without,"[1] he does not do away with a careful and exact scrutiny, nor does he set up this testimony as a chief sign of assurance about such men. But having listed many requirements already, he added this one afterwards, to show that we must not be content with it alone for this kind of election, but only take it into account along with other considerations. For it often happens that popular report is false. But when a careful scrutiny has led the way, we need not suspect any danger from it. So he adds it—the opinion of those outside the Church—after the other kinds of evidence. He did not say absolutely, "He must have a good testimony," but he added the word "also", because he wanted to show that before adducing the report of those who are outside, we must examine the man himself with care. Since, then, I myself knew your character better than your own parents, as you yourself admitted, I deserve to be acquitted of all blame.

Basil: That is the very reason why you would not have been let off, if anyone had wanted to accuse you. Or do you not remember having often heard me say and show by my actions how mean my spirit is? Were you not for ever jeering at my small-mindedness, because I so easily gave way to commonplace worries?

John: I do remember often hearing you say so, and I will not deny it. But if I ever jeered at you, I did so in fun, not in earnest. However, I will not argue about that now. But I beg you to show me the same forbearance when I want to call to remembrance some of the good qualities you possess.

[1] 1 Tim. 3.7.

For if you try to prove that I am not telling the truth, I shall not spare you, but I shall demonstrate that you are just making a pretence and not speaking for the truth's sake. And I shall use your own words and actions as evidence of what I say.

But first I want you to tell me this: do you know the power of love? Christ passed over all the marvellous works which were to be performed by the apostles and said, "By this shall men know that ye are my disciples, if ye love one another."[2] And Paul says that love is the fulfilment of the law,[3] and that without it spiritual gifts profit nothing.[4] This then, the chief of virtues, the talisman of Christ's disciples, the highest of all spiritual gifts, this I saw was truly implanted in your spirit and teeming with fruit.

Basil: I confess myself that I give much thought to this matter and take great pains over this commandment. But I have not half fulfilled it, as you yourself might testify, if you would stop paying compliments and give the truth its due.

John: Very well, then, I will turn to the evidence. I shall do what I threatened and prove that you meant to disparage yourself rather than speak the truth. I shall mention something that happened recently, to prevent anyone suspecting that by relating far-off things I am trying to obscure the truth through long lapse of time, since forgetfulness would then preclude any denunciation of my compliments to you.

When one of our friends had been wrongfully accused on a charge of insolent and presumptuous conduct and was in the utmost danger, then although no one made any charge against you, and the man in imminent danger made no appeal to you, you threw yourself into the midst of the peril. That was what you did. But, to convict you from your words as well, you said to your critics (since there were some who

[2] Cf. John 13.35.   [3] Rom. 13.10.   [4] 1 Cor. 13.3.

did not approve of your concern, though others praised and admired it), "What am I to do? I know no other meaning for friendship but that which carries the offer of my own life, when one of my friends in danger needs to be saved." That was to repeat in other words, but with the same meaning, Christ's saying to his disciples, when he defined perfect love. "Greater love," he said, "hath no man than this, that a man lay down his life for his friends."[5] If, then, no greater love than this can be found, you have already reached its perfection. By what you did and what you said, you scaled its summit. That is why I betrayed you. That is why I wove my web of deceit. Have I convinced you that I dragged you into this arena, not from ill-will or the desire to put you in danger, but because I knew that you would do good work?

Basil: Then do you think that the power of love is enough to enable a man to direct his neighbours?

John: Certainly it goes a long way towards it. But if you want me to give examples of your wisdom as well, I will proceed to that, and show that you are even more wise than loving.

Basil (colouring up and blushing at this) : Suppose we let my character alone now! At the outset I did not ask you to give an account of it. But if you have any reasonable answer to give to outsiders, I should be glad to hear it from you. So stop this shadow-boxing, and tell me what answer to make, both to those who honoured us and to those who are resentful on their behalf as though they had been insulted.

[5] John 15.13.

6

JOHN CONTINUES HIS APOLOGIA

JOHN: Yes, I am myself anxious to come to that. Now that I have finished the explanation of my conduct towards you, I shall be glad to turn to that part of my defence. What, then, is their accusation? What are the charges?

Basil: They say that they have been insulted and shamefully treated by us, because we would not receive the honour which they wanted to bestow on us.

John: My first point is this: we must not mind insulting men, if by respecting them we offend God. Even for these people who are resentful it is not safe to be offended at a refusal; it does them a great deal of harm. For I think that men who are consecrated to God and look to him alone, ought to be so reverent in their disposition as not to consider treatment of this kind an insult, even if they were slighted over and over again.

But it is quite obvious that I did not dare even to think of doing any such thing, and for this reason. If it was through arrogance and vainglory (as you said some people often slanderously assert) that I came to the point of confirming their accusations, I should be a first-class offender for treating with contempt persons of note and eminence, who were, moreover, my own benefactors. For if we deserve punishment for wronging those who have done no wrong to us, what penalty could be too severe for requiting with the very opposite of honour those who chose to honour us spontaneously? For no one could say that they had received any favours, great or small, from me, and so were requiting me for kindnesses which I had shown them. But if that idea never occurred to me; if I had another reason for avoiding such a heavy burden, why do they refuse to forgive, if they cannot approve? Why do they accuse me because I was merciful to my own soul? I was so far from insulting the men in question, that I should say I have done them honour by my refusal. Do not be surprised if my statement sounds a paradox. I shall quickly explain it.

If I had done otherwise, everybody (or at least those who take pleasure in backbiting) would have been able to make many suspicious remarks about me for being elected and about those who appointed me; as, for example, that they had an eye to wealth or were admirers of an illustrious family or that they had been flattered by me and so had brought my name forward. I do not know whether some might not have suspected that they had been bribed. Or again, "Christ called fishermen and tentmakers and tax-collectors to this office. But these people scorn men who live by their daily toil and accept and admire anyone who devotes himself to secular studies and lives at leisure. Why else did they pass over those who have undertaken innumerable hard tasks to meet the needs of the Church? Why else did they suddenly drag into this dignity a man who had never tasted that kind of hard work but had spent his youth in the vanity of secular studies?"

All this and more they might have said, if I had accepted the office. But they cannot now. Every pretext for slander has been removed. They cannot accuse me of flattery nor these others of corruption, unless they want to act like fools. For how could a man who had flattered and bribed to gain office have resigned the honour to others when he should have received it himself? It would be like a man working hard on his farm to make sure his cornfield stood thick with

a heavy crop and his presses overflowed with wine, and then
after his hard work and heavy expense, when the time came
to harvest the corn and the grapes, leaving it to others to
reap the fruit! Do you see that in the one case, however
wide of the mark their words might be, still those who
wanted to slander them could have found a pretext to do so,
on the grounds that they had made their choice by a crooked
assessment of the arguments? But as it is, I have not let them
open their mouths wide or even utter a sound. Yet all this
and more they would have said from the start.

After entering on my ministry I should not have been
able to answer their daily accusations, even if all my actions
had been perfect—not to allow for my many inevitable
mistakes due to inexperience and youth. As it is, I have
cleared these others of this slander. But otherwise I should
have brought upon them a load of reproaches. What would
people not have said? "They have entrusted foolish boys
with matters so sacred and important. They have outraged
the flock of Christ. Christianity has been made a joke and a
laughing stock!" But now "all iniquity shall stop her
mouth".[1] For if they say this on your account, you at least
will soon teach them by your actions not to measure
understanding by age, nor judge an old man by his grey
hairs, nor debar the young man altogether from so high an
office, but only the novice—and there is a great difference
between the two.

Such then is the reply I should give in answer to the
charge of insulting those who would have honoured me, and
to prove that in refusing this dignity, I had no wish to bring
disgrace on them. Now I will try, to the best of my ability,
to prove to you that I was not puffed up with conceit.

If the offer of a generalship or a kingdom had been made

[1] Ps. 107.42.

to me, and if I had then made the same decision, someone might possibly have suspected it. Or, more probably, everyone would have judged me not conceited but mad. But when what is offered is the priesthood, which is as far superior to a kingdom as spirit is to flesh, will anyone dare to accuse me of contempt? Is it not absurd to accuse of madness people who refuse small honours, but, when they do the same with regard to very great honours, to drop the charge of madness and substitute accusations of pride? It is like accusing a man of insanity and not conceit, because he despised a herd of cattle and would not be a cowherd, but saying he was guilty, not of madness but of extreme pride, if he refused the kingdom of the whole world and the generalship of all armies everywhere.

This will not do; it will not do! To talk like that is to disparage themselves, not us. Merely to think that it is possible for human nature to despise that dignity shows the opinion of the office held by the people who express that idea. If they did not regard it as commonplace and unimportant, such a suspicion would never have occurred to them. Why has no one ever dared to suspect or suggest the idea about the dignity of angels, that through pride the human soul refuses to accept the dignity of their order? We form a high conception of those powerful beings, and this prevents us believing that man could imagine anything greater than that dignity. And so those who accuse us of conceit might be more fairly accused of it themselves. For they would never have suspected it in others, if they had not themselves despised the office already as insignificant.

And if they say that my action was caused by ambition they will be proved to contradict themselves and to confound themselves plainly. Indeed I do not know what argument they could better have chosen if they had wanted to

clear me of the charge of vainglory. For if that motive had
ever entered my head, I should have been sure to accept the
office, not decline it. Why? Because it would have brought
me great credit. If anyone as young as myself, having only
just abandoned worldly pursuits, were suddenly reckoned by
everyone so marvellous as to be preferred to those who had
spent all their life in similar work and to receive more votes
than any of them, it would have made everyone suspect that
I had some great and wonderful qualities and would have
given me an august and distinguished reputation. But as it
is, the great majority of the Church, with few exceptions, do
not even know me by name. So my refusal is not known to
all, but only to a few, and even they, I believe, do not all
know the facts. Probably many of them thought either that
I was not chosen at all or that I was rejected as unsuitable
after being chosen, and not that I voluntarily refused the
office.

Basil: But those who know the truth will admire your
action.

John: And yet you said that they were accusing me of
vainglory and pride! From whom, then, can I expect this
praise? From the many? But they do not know the facts.
Well, then, from the few? But there your argument has
turned completely round. For the only reason you have
come here now is to learn what answer you should give
them. Why am I arguing so carefully about them now?
Wait a moment and you will see quite clearly that, even if
everyone had known the truth, they need not have convicted
me of conceit or vainglory; and something else as well : that
there is great danger involved not only in daring to take this
attitude, but also in suspecting it in others.

7

THE GLORY OF THE PRIESTHOOD

THE WORK of the priesthood is done on earth, but it is
ranked among heavenly ordinances. And this is only right,
for no man, no angel, no archangel, no other created power,
but the Paraclete himself ordained this succession, and persuaded men, while still remaining in the flesh to represent the
ministry of angels. The priest, therefore, must be as pure as
if he were standing in heaven itself, in the midst of those
powers.

The symbols which existed before the ministry of grace
were fearful and awe-inspiring : for example, the bells, the
pomegranates, the stones on the breastplate, the stones on
the ephod, the mitre, the diadem, the long robe, the golden
crown, the Holy of Holies, the deep silence within. But if
you consider the ministry of grace, you will find that those
fearful and awe-inspiring symbols are only trivial. The statement about the Law is true here also : "The splendour that
once was is now no splendour at all; it is outshone by a
splendour greater still."[1] When you see the Lord sacrificed
and lying before you, and the High Priest standing over the
sacrifice and praying, and all who partake being tinctured
with that precious blood, can you think that you are still
among men and still standing on earth? Are you not at once
transported to heaven, and, having driven out of your soul
every carnal thought, do you not with soul naked and mind
pure look round upon heavenly things? Oh, the wonder of
it ! Oh, the loving-kindness of God to men ! He who sits

[1] 2 Cor. 3.10 (N.E.B.).

above with the Father is at that moment held in our hands, and gives himself to those who wish to clasp and embrace him—which they do, all of them, with their eyes. Do you think this could be despised? or that it is the kind of thing anyone can be superior about?

Would you like to be shown the excellence of this sacred office by another miracle? Imagine in your mind's eye, if you will, Elijah and the vast crowd standing around him and the sacrifice lying upon the stone altar. All the rest are still, hushed in deep silence. The prophet alone is praying. Suddenly fire falls from the skies on to the offering. It is marvellous; it is charged with bewilderment. Turn, then, from that scene to our present rites, and you will see not only marvellous things, but things that transcend all terror. The priest stands bringing down, not fire, but the Holy Spirit. And he offers prayer at length, not that some flame lit from above may consume the offerings, but that grace may fall on the sacrifice through that prayer, set alight the souls of all, and make them appear brighter than silver refined in the fire. Can anyone, not quite mad and deranged, despise this most awe-inspiring rite? Do you not know that no human soul could ever have stood that sacrificial fire, but all would have been utterly annihilated, except for the powerful help of God's grace?

Anyone who considers how much it means to be able, in his humanity, still entangled in flesh and blood, to approach that blessed and immaculate Being, will see clearly how great is the honour which the grace of the Spirit has bestowed on priests. It is through them that this work is performed, and other work no less than this in its bearing upon our dignity and our salvation.

For earth's inhabitants, having their life in this world, have been entrusted with the stewardship of heavenly things, and have received an authority which God has not given to angels or archangels. Not to them was it said, "What things soever ye shall bind on earth shall be bound also in heaven; and what things soever ye shall loose, shall be loosed."[2] Those who are lords on earth have indeed the power to bind, but only men's bodies. But this binding touches the very soul and reaches through heaven. What priests do on earth, God ratifies above. The Master confirms the decisions of his slaves. Indeed he has given them nothing less than the whole authority of heaven. For he says, "Whose soever sins ye forgive, they are forgiven, and whose soever sins ye retain, they are retained."[3] What authority could be greater than that? "The Father hath given all judgement unto the Son."[4] But I see that the Son has placed it all in their hands. For they have been raised to this prerogative, as though they were already translated to heaven and had transcended human nature and were freed from our passions.

Again, if a king confers on one of his subjects the right to imprison and release again at will, that man is the envy and admiration of all. But although the priest has received from God an authority as much greater than that, as heaven is more precious than earth and souls than bodies, some people think he has received so slight an honour that they can imagine someone entrusted with it actually despising the gift. God save us from such madness! For it is patently mad to despise this great office without which we cannot attain to salvation or God's good promises.

For if a man "cannot enter into the kingdom of heaven except he be born again of water and the spirit,"[5] and if he that eateth not the Lord's flesh and drinketh not his blood

[2] Cf. Matt. 18.18.   [3] John 20.23.   [4] John 5.22.   [5] John 3.5.

is cast out of everlasting life,[6] and all these things can happen through no other agency except their sacred hands (the priests', I mean), how can anyone, without their help, escape the fire of Gehenna or win his appointed crown? They are the ones—they and no others—who are in charge of spiritual travail and responsible for the birth that comes through baptism. Through them we put on Christ and are united with the Son of God and become limbs obedient to that blessed Head. So they should properly be not only more feared than rulers and kings, but more honoured even than fathers. For our fathers begot us "of blood and the will of the flesh"; but they are responsible for our birth from God, that blessed second birth, our true emancipation, the adoption according to grace.

The priests of the Jews had authority to cure leprosy of the body, or rather, not to cure it, but only to certify the cure. And you know what rivalry there used to be for the priesthood then. But our priests have received authority not over leprosy of the body but over uncleanness of the soul, and not just to certify its cure, but actually to cure it. So people who look down on them are far more execrable than Dathan and his company and deserve more punishment. For although they claimed an office which did not belong to them, at least they had a marvellous opinion of it, as they showed by wanting it so much. But the people we are considering have done just the opposite at a time when the priesthood has been so embellished and enhanced. Their presumption, therefore, is far greater. In the assessment of contempt there is no comparison between coveting an honour which does not belong to you and making light of it. Between one and the other there is all the difference between admiration and disdain. Who could be so beggarly-minded

[6] Cf. John 6.53.

73

as to make light of these great blessings? No one, I should say, except the victim of some demonic impulse.

But, to return to the topic from which I digressed, God has given greater power to priests than to natural parents, not only for punishment, but also for help. The difference between the two is as great as between the present and the future life. Parents bring us into this life; priests into the life to come. Parents cannot avert bodily death nor drive away the onset of disease; priests have often saved the soul that is sick and at the point of death, by making the punishment milder for some, and preventing others from ever incurring it, not only through instruction and warning, but also through helping them by prayer. They have authority to remit sins, not only when they make us regenerate, but afterwards too. "Is any among you sick? Let him call for the elders of the Church, and let them pray over him, anointing him with oil in the name of the Lord. And the prayer of faith shall save him that is sick, and the Lord shall raise him up, and if he have committed sins, they shall be forgiven him."[7] Again, natural parents cannot help their sons if they fall foul of the prominent and powerful, but priests have often appeased the anger of God himself, to say nothing of rulers and kings.

Will anyone still dare to accuse me of arrogance after this? I think that after what I have said, such reverence must fill the minds of my hearers that they can no longer accuse of conceit and presumption those who avoid this honour, but only those who seek it of their own accord and are determined to get it for themselves.

[7] Jas. 5.14–15.

8

THE DIFFICULTY OF THE PRIESTHOOD

IF IT is true that those who are entrusted with civic government subvert their cities and ruin themselves as well, unless they are wise and very watchful, what about the man whose task is to adorn the bride of Christ? How much strength in himself and from above do you think he needs to avoid complete failure?

No one loved Christ more than Paul; no one showed more earnestness than he; no one was endowed with more grace. Yet for all that he went in fear and trembling for his authority and those who were under it. He says, "I fear lest, as the serpent beguiled Eve, so your thoughts should be corrupted from the simplicity which is towards Christ." [1] And again, "I was with you in fear and in much trembling." [2] Yet he was a man who had been "caught up to the third heaven",[3] and shared in the unspeakable things of God,[4] and endured "deaths"[5] every day he lived after his conversion. He was a man who did not want to use the authority given him by Christ in case one of the believers should be offended.[6]

If, then, one who did more than he was commanded by God and never aimed at any advantage for himself, but only for those under his direction, was always in fear, because he kept in view the magnitude of his responsibility, what will become of us, who often aim at our own advantage, and, so far from doing more than we are commanded by Christ, for

[1] 2 Cor. 11.3. [2] 1 Cor. 2.3. [3] 2 Cor. 12.2.
[4] Cf. 2 Cor. 12.4. [5] 2 Cor. 11.23. [6] 1 Cor. 9.12.

the most part actually break his commandments? "Who is weak", he says, "and I am not weak? Who is made to stumble, and I burn not?"[7] That is what a priest should be like; or rather, not just like that, for even that is little or nothing in comparison with what I am going to say.

And what is that? "I could wish," he says, "that I were anathema from Christ for my brethren's sake, my kinsmen according to the flesh."[8] If anyone can say that; if anyone has a soul capable of that prayer, he would be to blame if he evaded the priesthood. But anyone who falls as far short of that standard as I do, deserves hatred, not for evading but for accepting it.

If it were a question of choosing someone for a generalship, and those responsible for conferring the honour dragged forward a coppersmith or a cobbler or some other workman of that sort, and tried to put him in charge of the army, I should not congratulate the poor man for not running off and doing all he could to avoid pitching himself into inevitable disaster.

If it is enough simply to be called a "shepherd of souls" and to undertake the work anyhow, without risk, blame me for vainglory if you like. But if, on the contrary, the man who accepts this responsibility needs great wisdom and, even before wisdom, the grace of God in good measure, and an upright character and a pure life, and more than human goodness, then do not withhold your forgiveness from me because I do not want to damn myself without rhyme or reason.

Suppose someone brought a merchant ship of great tonnage, fully equipped with rowers and loaded with valuable freight, and sat me at the rudder and told me to cross the Aegean or the Tyrrhenian Sea, I should jump off at his first

[7] 2 Cor. 11.29.   [8] Rom. 9.3.

words. And if anybody asked me why, I should say, "To save sinking the ship!" When it is only money that is at stake, and the risk is at most of bodily death, no one will blame a man for looking well ahead. But where the fate of the shipwrecked is to fall, not into the sea, but into the abyss of fire, and what awaits them is not the death which separates soul from body, but the death which consigns both together to eternal punishment, will you be angry with me and hate me for not throwing myself headlong into such a calamity? I beg and beseech you not to. I know how weak and puny my own soul is. I know the importance of that ministry and the great difficulty of it. More billows toss the priest's soul than the gales which trouble the sea.

First of all there is the dreadful rock of vainglory, more dangerous than the Sirens' rock of which the poets have marvellous tales to tell. Many have had the strength to sail past this rock and escape unscathed. But to me it is so dangerous that even now, when no necessity is driving me towards its cleft, I cannot keep myself untainted by the terrible thing. If anyone entrusted this charge to me, he would be as good as binding my hands behind my back and delivering me to the wild beasts that inhabit that rock, to savage me every day. And what are those beasts? Anger, dejection, envy, strife, slanders, accusations, lying, hypocrisy, intrigue, imprecations against those who have done no harm, delight at disgraceful behaviour in fellow priests, sorrow at their successes, love of praise, greed for preferment (which more than anything else hurls the human soul to destruction), teaching meant to please, slavish wheedling, ignoble flattery, contempt for the poor, fawning on the rich, absurd honours and harmful favours which endanger giver and receiver alike, servile fear fit only for the meanest of slaves, restraint of plain speaking, much pretended and no real humility, failure to scrutinize and rebuke, or, more likely, doing so beyond reason with the humble while no one dares so much as to open his lips against those who wield power. All these wild beasts and more are bred upon that rock. And people who are once seized by them cannot help being dragged into the kind of servitude which makes them do over and over again, even to please women, things that are too bad to mention.

The divine law excluded women from this ministry, but they forcibly push themselves in, and, since they can do nothing personally, they do everything by proxy. They have got such power that they appoint and dismiss priests at will. Topsy-turvy (you can see the truth of the proverb borne out) "the followers lead their leaders"—bad enough, if they were men; but they are women, the very ones who are not even allowed to teach. Do I say "teach"? St Paul did not allow them even to speak in church.[9] But I have heard it said that they have assumed such freedom of speech that they even rebuke the prelates of the churches and upbraid them more bitterly than masters would their slaves.

But do not let anyone think that I am bringing these charges against all the clergy. Many there certainly are who have escaped these entanglements—more indeed than those who have been caught in them. And I do not venture to blame the priestly office for these evils. God forbid that I should be such a fool! Wise men do not blame the knife for murder, nor wine for drunkenness, nor strength for insolence, nor courage for recklessness. No; they blame the men who make wrong use of the gifts of God, and punish them for it. The priestly office might well accuse us of not handling it rightly. It is not itself the cause of the evils I have mentioned. It is we on our part who have smirched it

[9] 1 Cor. 14.34.

with stain upon stain, by entrusting it to commonplace men. And they eagerly accept what is offered to them, without first examining their own souls or considering the gravity of the matter. And when they come to exercise this ministry, their eyes are blinded with inexperience and they fill the congregations entrusted to them with a thousand and one troubles.

That was the very thing that all but happened to me— only that God quickly rescued me from these dangers, in mercy on his Church and on my soul. Tell me, where do you think all the disorders in the churches originate? I think their only origin is in the careless and random way in which the prelates are chosen and appointed. For the head ought to be the strongest member, in order to be able to control the evil exhalations which proceed from the rest of the body, and regulate them properly. But when it happens to be weak in itself, it cannot ward off those infectious attacks, becomes weaker than it naturally is, and destroys the rest of the body along with itself. To prevent this happening in the present instance, God has kept me safely in the category of "feet"—where I originally belonged!

9

THE CHARACTER AND TEMPTATIONS OF A BISHOP

THERE ARE many other qualities, Basil, in addition to those I have mentioned, which a priest ought to have, and which I lack. And the first of all is that he must purify his soul entirely of ambition for the office. For if he is strongly attracted to this office, when he gets it he will add fuel to the fire and, being mastered by ambition, he will tolerate all kinds of evil to secure his hold upon it, even resorting to flattery, or submitting to mean and unworthy treatment, or spending lavishly. I pass over for the moment, for fear of seeming to say things beyond credit, the fact that some men, in contending for this office, have filled the churches with murder and split cities into factions.

The right course, I think, is to have so reverent an estimation of the office as to avoid its responsibility from the start; and, after being appointed to it, not to wait for the judgement of others, if you should happen to have committed a sin that calls for deposition, but to anticipate this and depose yourself from office. In this way a man will probably induce God's mercy. But if he clings to a position for which he is not fit, he deprives himself of all pardon and provokes God's anger the more by adding a second and more serious offence. But no one will ever be content to do so; for it is indeed a terrible temptation to covet this honour. And in saying this, I do not contradict St Paul, but entirely agree with what he says. What are his words? "If a man seeketh the office of a bishop, he desireth a good work."[1] I meant it was terrible to desire, not the work, but the absolute authority and power.

I think a man must rid his mind of this ambition with all possible care, and not for a moment let it be governed by it, in order that he may always act with freedom. For if he does not want to achieve fame in this position of authority, he will not dread its loss either. And if he does not fear this, he can always act with the freedom which befits Christian men. But those who fear and dread deposition from this office endure a bitter slavery, full of all kinds of evil, and cannot help often offending man and God.

But the soul ought not to be in this condition. As in war we see soldiers of fine spirit fighting eagerly and falling bravely, so those who have come to this administration should be ready either to be consecrated to the office or to be relieved of it, as befits Christian men, knowing that such deposition earns a crown no less than the office itself.

For when anyone has this done to him because he will not submit to anything which is unbecoming or unworthy of his position, he procures a greater punishment for those who wrongfully depose him, and a greater reward for himself. "Blessed are ye," says our Lord, "when men shall reproach you and persecute you, and say all manner of evil against you falsely for my sake. Rejoice and be exceeding glad; for great is your reward in heaven."[2] This is surely true even when anyone is expelled by men of his own order, either through envy or to please others or through enmity or any other wrong motive. But when he gets this treatment from his enemies, I do not think any argument is needed to prove how great a benefit they confer on him by their wickedness.

So we must be thoroughly on our guard against ambition and examine ourselves carefully to prevent a spark of it from

[1] I Tim. 3.1.   [2] Matt. 5.11–12.

smouldering anywhere unseen. It is much to be desired that those who at first were free from this infection should be able to keep clear of it when they have entered office. But if anyone nurtures within himself this terrible, savage beast before attaining office, there is no telling what a furnace he will fling himself into, after he has attained it. For my own part (and do not think that I would ever lie to you out of self-depreciation), I possess this ambition in a high degree. And this fact, quite as much as all the other reasons, alarmed me and impelled me to run away as I did. For just as lovers of a human person endure a terrible torment of passion as long as they can be near the objects of their love, but throw off their frenzy when they take themselves as far away as possible from those whom they desire; so also those who covet this office find the evil intolerable while they are near it, but quench the desire along with the expectation, as soon as they give up hope.

This, then, was one strong motive, and even if it had been all by itself, it would have been enough to debar me from this dignity. In fact, however, there is another motive quite as strong. What is it? A priest must be sober and clear-sighted and possess a thousand eyes looking in every direction, for he lives, not for himself alone, but for a great multitude. But I am sluggish and remiss and scarcely sufficient for my own salvation, as even you should admit, though you are most of all eager to hide my faults for love's sake.

Do not speak to me now of fasting and vigils and sleeping on the ground and other bodily discipline. You know how far short I come even in these. But if these exercises had been most carefully regulated by me, they would have been unable to equip me at all for this responsibility, while my sluggishness remained. They would be a great help to someone shut up in a cell and concerned only about his own soul. But when a man is distracted by such a huge multitude and inherits all the private cares of those who are under his rule, what appreciable help can these practices contribute towards their improvement, unless he has a healthy, robust soul?

Do not be surprised if, in addition to such endurance, I apply another touchstone of spiritual strength. We can see that contempt for food and drink and soft bedding comes easily to many, especially to more uncouth natures brought up in that way from early childhood, but to many others as well. For bodily constitution and practice mitigate the severity of those exercises. But there are not many, indeed only one or two here and there, who can bear insult and abuse and vulgar language and taunts from inferiors, spoken casually or deliberately, and complaints made at random by the rulers and the ruled. You see men who are valiant in ascetic practices so far losing their heads at these that they become wilder than savage beasts. We must debar such men in particular from the precincts of the priesthood. For it would not harm the common life of the Church if a prelate should neither starve himself of food, nor go barefoot. But a furious temper causes great disasters both to its possessor and to his neighbours. There is no threat from God against those who omit these ascetic practices, but those who are angry without a cause are threatened with hell and hell fire.[3] As, then, the lover of vainglory adds fresh fuel to the fire when he assumes the government of numbers, so a man who cannot control his temper while alone or in the company of a few others, but is easily thrown into a passion, is like a wild beast baited by crowds all round, when he is entrusted with the rule of an entire congregation. He cannot live at peace

[3] Cf. Matt. 5.22.

himself and spreads evils galore among the people committed to his charge.

Nothing muddies the purity of the mind and the perspicacity of the wits as much as an ungovernable temper that fluctuates violently. Scripture says, "This destroys even the prudent."[4] For the soul's eye is darkened, as in a night battle, and cannot distinguish friend from foe or worthless from worthy. It treats all in turn alike (even though some evil consequence ensues), carelessly accepting every consequence to gratify the soul's pleasure, even if it means a crop of trouble. For a blazing temper is a kind of pleasure, and it tyrannizes over the soul more harshly than pleasure, thoroughly upsetting all its healthy condition. It easily excites men to insolence, to ill-timed enmities and unreasonable hatred, and is for ever making them give wilful offence and forcing them to say and do many other things just as bad. For the soul is swept along with the strong rush of passion and has no base on which to rest its own strength and resist so strong an attack.

Basil: I will not put up with your humbug any longer. Who knows better than I how free you are from this disease?

John: Why, then, my dear fellow, do you want to drag me near the pyre and bait the sleeping beast? Do you not know that my freedom from this fault is due, not to my innate goodness, but to my love of retirement? It is good for anyone in this condition (not to mention anyone who has fallen into the very abyss of heavy anxieties) to remain by himself or keep company with one or two friends, and so manage to avoid being set on fire with this passion. For otherwise he drags, not himself only, but many others with him, to the brink of ruin, and makes them more careless

[4] Prov. 15.1 (LXX).

84

about the cultivation of a gentle character. For the mass of people under government are, for the most part, prone to regard the character of their rulers as a kind of archetype, and to assimilate themselves to it. And how can anyone stop their outbursts, if he is excitable himself? What ordinary man would naturally want to learn self-control when he sees his ruler is hot-tempered?

The priest's shortcomings simply cannot be concealed. On the contrary, even the most trivial soon get known. The weakest athlete can keep his weakness secret as long as he remains at home and pits himself against nobody; but when he strips for the contest, he is soon shown up. So with other men : those who lead a retired and inactive life have their solitude as a cloak for their private faults; but when they are brought into public life, they are compelled to strip off their retirement like a garment and to show everyone their naked souls by their outward movements. As, then, their right actions benefit many and challenge them to equal efforts, so their faults make other men careless in the quest of virtue, and encourage them to shirk hard work for the things that matter. Therefore the beauty of his soul must shine out brightly all round, to be able to gladden and enlighten the souls of those who see.

The sins of ordinary men are committed in the dark, so to speak, and ruin only those who commit them. But when a man becomes famous and is known to many, his misdeeds inflict a common injury on all. They make backsliders even more supine in their efforts for what is good, and drive to despair those who want to improve. Apart from this, the offences of the insignificant, even if made public, harm no one seriously. But those who are set upon the pinnacle of this honour not only catch every eye; more than that, however trifling their offences, these little things seem great to others, since everyone measures sin, not by the size of the offence, but by the standing of the sinner.

The priest must be armed with weapons of steel—intense earnestness and constant sobriety of life—and he must keep watch in every direction, in case anyone should find a naked and unguarded spot and strike him a mortal blow. For everyone stands round him ready to wound him and strike him down, not only his enemies and foes, but many of those who pretend to love him. We must, therefore, choose souls as hardy as God's grace once proved the bodies of the saints in the Babylonian furnace.[5] The fuel of this fire is not brushwood, pitch, and tow, but something far worse than that. It is no material fire to which they are exposed, but the all-devouring flame of malice envelops them, rising up all round, and attacking them and searching their life more thoroughly than the fire did the bodies of those young men. When it finds the slightest trace of stubble, it quickly lays hold of it and burns up the rotten part, while all the rest of the building, even though brighter than rays of sunshine, is scorched and blackened completely by the smoke.

For as long as the priest's life is well regulated in every particular point, their intrigues cannot hurt him. But if he should overlook some small detail, as is likely for a human being on his journey across the devious ocean of this life, all the rest of his good deeds are of no avail to enable him to escape the words of his accusers. That small offence casts a shadow over all the rest of his life. Everyone wants to judge the priest, not as one clothed in flesh, not as one possessing a human nature, but as an angel, exempt from the frailty of others.

Everyone fears and flatters a tyrant as long as his power lasts, because they cannot depose him. But when they see his

[5] Dan. 3.27.

power decline, those who were just now his friends throw off their hypocritical esteem and suddenly become his foes and enemies. When they have discovered all his weaknesses, they set upon him and depose him from power. So it is with priests. Those who but now flattered and courted him when he was in power, once they have found the least handle, eagerly make plans to depose him, not merely as a tyrant, but as something far worse than that. Again, as a tyrant fears his bodyguard, so he dreads above all his neighbours and fellow ministers. For other people do not covet a tyrant's power as much, nor, above all, know his business as well, as these men know his. Being close to him, they learn before others of any faults that may occur. If they slander him, they can easily gain credence, and if they exaggerate trifles, they can convict the victim of their pettifogging. For the well-known saying of the Apostle has been inverted : "And if one member suffereth, all the members rejoice; and if one member is honoured, all the members suffer," [6] unless by great discretion someone can survive it all.

Are you, then, sending me forth to such a terrible war? Did you judge my spirit adequate for so complex and intricate a battle? Where did you get the information? And from whom? If it was God who revealed it, show me the oracle, and I will obey. But if you cannot do so and are making a judgement from human opinion, then deceive yourself no longer. For you should believe me rather than others about myself, since "no man knoweth the things of a man, save the spirit of the man which is in him". [7]

With these arguments I think I must have persuaded you now, if not before, that I should have made both myself and those who chose me ridiculous by accepting this office, and that I should have returned again to the path of life in

[6] Contrast 1 Cor. 12.26.   [7] Cf. 1 Cor. 2.11.

which I now am, but at great cost. For it is not only malice, but something far worse than malice—ambition for office—that usually arms the majority of men against the one who possesses it. And as covetous sons begrudge their fathers a long life, so when some of these men see the priestly office held by anyone for a prolonged period, they are anxious to depose him, as it would hardly be right to murder him! For they are all ambitious to succeed him and everyone expects that the office will fall to himself.

10

PARTICULAR DUTIES AND PROBLEMS

1. *Promotions*

WOULD YOU like me to show you one more aspect of this contest which is full of innumerable dangers? Come and take a peep at the public festivals, at which it is the custom for most appointments to ecclesiastical office to be made. You will see the priest assailed with as many accusations as there are persons under his rule. For all who are qualified to bestow the honour are then split into many factions and the synod of presbyters can be seen agreeing neither among themselves nor with the one who has received the episcopal office. Each man stands alone. One chooses this candidate and another that. The reason is that they do not all concentrate on the one thing they should—spiritual worth. There are other considerations which influence appointment to office. For example, one man says, "Let this man be chosen, because he belongs to a distinguished family"; another says, "Because he possesses a large fortune and would not need supporting out of the Church's revenues"; another, "Because he is a convert from the other side". One man is anxious to promote above the rest a friend, another a relative, another someone who flatters him. No one will look for the best qualified man or apply any spiritual test.

I myself, so far from thinking these are worthy grounds for approving priests, should not dare to select a man quickly, even if he showed great piety (though to me it is no small qualification for that office), unless he combined with piety considerable intelligence as well. For I know many

who have kept themselves under discipline all their life and
exhausted their bodies with fasting, and who, as long as
they were allowed to live alone and attend to their own
needs, were acceptable to God and every day made great
progress in this philosophy. Yet when they returned to normal society and had to correct the follies of the common
people, they either did not begin to cope with so great a
responsibility, or else, when compelled to remain at their
post, abandoned their former high standards, brought a
heavy penalty on themselves and were not of the least use
to others.

Again, if a man has spent all his life in the lowest order
of the ministry and has reached extreme old age, we will
not, simply out of respect for his age, promote him to the
next order. What if he should still be unsuitable, even after
a lifetime? I do not say this out of disrespect for grey hairs,
nor am I laying down a rule that we should entirely exclude
from such responsibility those who come from the monastic
fraternity. It has turned out that many even from that body
have shed lustre upon this office. But I am anxious to show
that, if neither piety by itself nor old age alone are sufficient
to prove a man worthy of the priesthood, the reasons I have
mentioned are hardly likely to do so.

Other people go on to give reasons which are stranger
still. Some are enlisted in the ranks of the clergy to prevent
their siding with the enemy, and others because of their bad
character, to stop them causing a lot of trouble if they are
overlooked! Could any worse violation of the right take
place than that corrupt men, replete with vices, should be
courted for the very things for which they ought to be
punished, and promoted to priestly dignity for the very
things for which they ought to be forbidden to cross the
threshold of the Church? Tell me, do we need to look any

further for the cause of God's anger, when we expose the most sacred and awe-inspiring things to defilement by wicked or worthless men? When some men are entrusted with things unsuited to them and others with things quite beyond their powers, they make the Church as unstable as the Euripus.

I once used to deride secular rulers because they distributed honours, not on grounds of inherent merit, but of wealth or seniority or worldly rank. But when I heard that this stupidity had swaggered into our own affairs too, I no longer reckoned their action so strange. For why should we be surprised that worldly people, who love the praise of the mob and do everything for money, should make this mistake, when those who claim to have renounced all these desires are no better? For although they are contending for heavenly rewards, they act as though they had to decide merely about acres of land or something else of the kind. They simply take commonplace men and put them in charge of those things for which the only-begotten Son of God did not disdain to empty himself of his own glory and to be made man and to receive the form of a servant and to be spitted upon and buffeted and to die the most shameful death.

And they do not stop at this, but go on to other actions stranger still. They not merely choose the unworthy; they reject those who are suitable. As though it were necessary to undermine the safety of the Church in both ways, or as though the first reason were not enough to kindle the wrath of God, they have added another reason no less serious. For I think it is as bad to keep out the capable as to bring in the useless. And this is done to prevent the flock of Christ from finding comfort or a breathing-space anywhere. Does not this deserve a hail of thunder-bolts? Does it not deserve some special hell and not just the one we are threatened with? Yet all these evils are suffered and borne patiently by the one who does not desire the death of a sinner, but rather that he should be converted and live. How can we marvel enough at his love for man, or wonder at his mercy? Christians damage Christ's cause more than his enemies and foes. But the good Lord still shows his kindness and calls us to repentance.

Glory be to thee, O Lord! Glory be to thee! What an abyss of love is in thee! How great are the riches of thy forbearance! Men who through thy Name have come to be worthy and respected instead of mean and worthless use that honour against thee who gavest it, and dare what is forbidden, and insult what is holy, rejecting and excluding the earnest, in order that evil men may have perfect freedom and full security to subvert whatever they desire.

If you want to know the reasons for this scandal, you will find they are like those I mentioned before. They have one root and, so to speak, one mother: malice. Yet they are not all of one kind, but different. One man says, "Reject him, because he is young"; another says, "Because he has not learnt how to flatter"; another, "Because he has offended so-and-so". Or again, someone says, "Reject him in case so-and-so should be hurt to see his own nominee rejected and this man appointed"; another says, "Reject him because he is good and just"; another, "Because sinners fear him"; and another gives some other such reason. They have ready to hand all the pretexts they require. Even the number of existing clergy is sufficient argument, when they have no better. Or they argue that it is advisable not to promote a man to this honour suddenly, but gently and by degrees. And they can find as many other reasons as they want.

But I should like to ask you now what a bishop ought

to do when he has to contend with so many winds. How can he stand firm against such great breakers? How can he repel all these attacks? If he settles the question by honest assessment, all men become enemies and foes to him and to those whom he has chosen. Everything they do is meant to create hostility to him. They stir up feuds daily and heap endless ridicule on those he has chosen, until they either depose them or get their own men in. It is like a captain having pirates sailing with him on board ship and continually plotting hour by hour against him and the sailors and crew. If, on the other hand, he prefers popularity with them to his own safety and so chooses unsuitable men, he will incur God's enmity in place of theirs. And what could be worse than that? And his relations with them will be more difficult than before, since they will all conspire together and become so much the stronger. When fierce winds meet from contrary quarters, the sea which before was quiet suddenly rages and towers, and destroys those who sail on it; so the calm sea of the Church, when evil men are accepted, is filled with surf and wreckage.

Consider, then, what qualities a man needs if he is to withstand such a tempest and deal successfully with these obstacles to the common good. He must be dignified yet modest, impressive yet kindly, masterful yet approachable, impartial yet courteous, humble but not servile, vehement yet gentle, in order that he may be able calmly to resist all these dangers and to promote a suitable man with full authority, even though everyone opposes him, and reject an unsuitable man with equal authority, even though everyone favours him. One thing alone he must consider : the edification of the Church. He must do nothing out of hostility or favour.

Well, then, do you think it was unreasonable to excuse

myself from serving in this capacity? And even yet I have
not made all my points to you; I have still more to say. So
do not lose patience with an intimate friend who wants to
convince you that he is clear of your imputations. For what
I say will not only be of service to you in my defence but
will probably afford considerable help towards your own
exercise of the office. For anyone who is about to enter upon
this walk of life needs to explore it all thoroughly beforehand and only then to undertake this ministry. And why?
Because if he studies the difficulties beforehand he will at
any rate have the advantage of not being taken by surprise
when they crop up.

2. *Widows and the Sick*

Would you like us, then, to pass on next to the super-
intendence of the widows, or the charge of the virgins, or the
difficulties of the judicial work? For in each of these there
is anxiety of a different kind and more danger than anxiety.

First, to begin with what appears to be easier than the
rest, the ministry to the widows seems to involve those who
are in charge of them only in responsibility of a financial
nature. But this is not so. On the contrary, here, too, close
scrutiny is needed when they are enrolled. Entering their
names carelessly and casually has led to untold troubles.
They have wrecked homes and broken marriages and often
been detected stealing and procuring and committing other
disgraceful offences like these. To support women like that
from Church funds brings down vengeance from God and
utter condemnation from men, and discourages those who
want to do good. For who would ever choose to spend the
money which he is commanded to give to Christ on those
who bring Christ's name into dishonour. That is why it is
necessary to make a long and precise scrutiny, to prevent

those whom I have described, as well as those who can provide for themselves, from plundering the table of those who cannot.

After this scrutiny there follows another big anxiety : to see that the means for their support should pour in abundantly, like water from a spring, and never fail. For involuntary poverty is an insatiable evil, querulous and unthankful. Great wisdom and plenty of energy are required to take away all occasion for complaint and stop their tongues wagging. When people see anyone superior to avarice, they at once point him out as suitable for this administration. But I do not think that honesty by itself is enough. You must look for it first of all, since without it a man will be a spoiler rather than a guardian and a wolf instead of a shepherd. But you must look for the possession of another quality as well, and that is forbearance, the source of all human blessings, which guides the soul to anchorage and escorts it into a fair haven.

Widows, as a class, owing partly to their poverty, partly to their age, and partly to their sex, use an unbridled freedom of speech—to call it no worse ! They scold out of season and find unnecessary fault and lament what they ought to be thankful for and criticize what they ought to welcome. The man in charge of them must bear it all politely and not be provoked by their inopportune fussing or their unreasonable complaints. For persons of this kind deserve to be pitied, not insulted, for their misfortunes. And it would be a mark of utter cruelty to take advantage of their misfortunes and add to the pain of poverty the pain of insult.

That is why a very wise man, observing the avarice and indifference of human nature, realized the terrible characteristic of poverty, that it debases the most generous soul and often teaches it to lose all shame on such matters. And so, to prevent anyone being angry when solicited by them and becoming their enemy when he ought to be their helper, because provoked by continual entreaty, he instructs us to be gentle and accessible to the needy, saying : "Incline thine ear to a poor man without grieving and answer him with peaceable words in meekness." [1] And ignoring those who provoke a man in distress—for what can you say to such sinners?—he speaks to anyone who can bear another's infirmity, urging him to help him up by kind looks and gentle words, before making a gift. If anyone should not actually take what is theirs but should load them with reproaches and insult them and be exasperated by them, he not only fails to relieve the desperation of poverty by his gift, but aggravates its misery by his abuse. For even if they are compelled by sheer hunger to be all too brazen, they are still hurt by this necessity. So when they are forced to beg by fear of starvation, and to be brazen by their begging, and are insulted because of their brazenness, the force of despondency which attacks them comes subtly and casts a deep gloom over them.

Whoever is in charge of them should be so long-suffering that, far from increasing their despondency by his own irritation, he actually soothes most of it away by his sympathy. For just as a rich man insulted forgets the benefit of his wealth through the pain of the insult, so one of these who hears a kindly word and receives a gift offered with sympathy, brightens up and is happy. The gift is doubled by the very manner of giving. I say this, not of myself, but on the authority of the writer whose advice I have quoted already. "My son," he says, "to thy good deeds add no blemish, and no grief of words in any of thy giving. Shall not the dew assuage the scorching heat? So is a word better than a gift.

[1] Ecclus. 4.8.

Lo, a word is better than a gift; and both are with a gracious man." [2]

The guardian of these people must be not only just and forbearing, but also a good steward. For if this quality is missing, the money of the poor is again exposed to equal risk of loss. Before now it has happened that someone entrusted with this ministry, and having collected a lot of money, has not wasted it on himself, but has not spent it on the needy either, except for a few; he has hidden and hoarded most of it until bad times have come and betrayed it into the hands of enemies. Much foresight, therefore, is needed to prevent the resources of the Church either piling up or running short. It is better to distribute all that is subscribed among the needy quickly and to lay up treasure for the Church in the good will of the congregation.

But what a lot of expense and care and thought, on the part of those in charge, is required for hospitality to strangers and the care of the sick! This is never less, and often more, than the expenditure I have already mentioned. The man in charge must be a discreet and shrewd treasurer, so as to encourage the wealthy to emulate one another and to give cheerfully of their substance. His object is to provide for the relief of the sick, without scourging the souls of the contributors. And here he must show outstanding forbearance and concern. Sick men are hard to please and given to languor. Unless every attention and care is lavished on them, the smallest neglect is enough to cause the patient great distress.

3. *Virgins*

As for the care of virgins, the anxiety is all the greater in proportion as the treasure is more precious, and this group is more like the Church's princesses than any other. Before

[2] Ecclus. 18.15–17.

now great numbers of women, full of innumerable vices, have intruded into the ranks of these holy ones. The grief for failure, too, is greater here. Just as it is not the same thing for a free-born girl and her servant to fall into sin, so it is not the same for a virgin and a widow. For it has become unremarkable for widows to gossip and to vilify each other and to flatter and to lose their self-respect and to be seen everywhere and to loiter about the market-place. But the virgin has prepared herself for a greater prize and devoted herself to the highest philosophy. She professes to display on earth the behaviour of the angels, and has the task of managing the concerns of such disembodied spirits while still living in the flesh. She must not walk abroad unnecessarily or often. She may not speak at all without good reason. She should not even know the meaning of abuse or flattery. And so she needs the closest watch and the greatest support. For the enemy of holiness is always marking them down and stalking them particularly, in readiness to swallow up any who stumble and fall—as do the many men who plot their downfall, and, to crown all, their own passionate natures. They have to arm themselves against a double attack, one launched from outside and the other mounting from within. And so their guardian has much anxiety and still more danger and distress, should anything undesirable happen (which God forbid!).

For if a daughter is "a secret cause of wakefulness to her father",[3] and his care for her makes him lose sleep through his great anxiety that she may be barren or pass her prime unmarried or be hated by her husband; what will a man feel whose anxiety is over none of these dangers, but others far greater than these? For here it is not a man who is disgraced, but Christ himself. And here barrenness does not just

[3] Ecclus. 42.9.

bring reproach, but the trouble ends in the soul's destruction. "For every tree," he says, "which bringeth not forth good fruit is hewn down and cast into the fire." [4] And if she is hated by the Bridegroom, it does not suffice to take a bill of divorcement and depart; but for that hatred he gives the punishment of eternal torment.

A natural father has many things that make it easy to watch over his daughter. For a mother and a nurse and plenty of maids and the security of the house help a father to guard the girl. She is not allowed to be perpetually dashing into the market-place. And when she does go, she is not compelled to show herself to anyone she meets, since the dusk of the evening conceals her no less than the walls of the house, if she does not want to be seen. And, apart from this, she is not answerable for herself, and so is never compelled to come into the presence of men; for neither concern for the necessities of life, nor the insults of wrong-doers, nor anything else like that, makes any such encounter necessary for her, since her father represents her in all capacities. But she herself has one care only : not to do or say anything unworthy of her proper modesty.

But in the case of a virgin, there are many circumstances that make it difficult, or rather, impossible, for her spiritual father to protect her. He cannot keep her at home with himself, since it would not be decent or safe to live together like that. For even if they themselves take no harm, but continue to keep their chastity undefiled, they will have to answer for the souls they lead astray, no less than if they had actually sinned against each other. Now since this arrangement is impossible, it is not easy to discover the shifts of her spirit, to check all that tends to disorder, and to train and improve all that is well-ordered and regular. Nor

[4] Matt. 3.10.

is it simple to interfere with her movements abroad. Her poverty and her independence do not permit him to be a close scrutineer of the decorum she ought to display. For since she is compelled to attend to all her own needs, she has many excuses for going out, if she wants to misbehave. So if someone orders her always to remain at home, he must take away these pretexts, make sufficient provision for her daily needs, and give her a woman to attend to them. She must also be forbidden funerals and vigils. For that subtle serpent knows very well how to spread his poison even by means of good deeds. The virgin must be completely immured, and must leave her house only a few times each year, when urgent necessity compels her.

Should any one say that it is not the bishop's job to attend to any of this, he must bear in mind that all particular anxieties and accusations are referred to him. It is much better for him to manage everything himself, and so be rid of the criticism which he must otherwise incur through the faults of others than to shed some particular ministry and go in fear of being called to account for what others do. Besides, if he does everything himself, he gets through all his business very easily. But if he has to do this and to persuade everyone else to agree as well, the relief he gets through freedom from personal labour is not equal to the trouble and bother he is caused by those who oppose him and resist his decisions.

But I cannot enumerate all the anxieties caused by virgins. The fact is that when they are enrolled they cause extraordinary trouble to the man who is entrusted with this administration.

4. Arbitration—Visiting—Excommunication

The judicial function involves innumerable burdens and

much expenditure of time, and greater difficulties even than those that face the judges in secular cases. It is a problem to find where justice lies, and it is hard not to pervert it when found. But expenditure of time and difficulty are not the only things involved; there is also no little danger. Before now some of the weaker brethren have got involved in disputes and, finding no favouritism, have "made shipwreck concerning the faith".[5] For many of those who have suffered wrong hate those who cannot help them just as much as those who did the wrong. They will not take into account the complicated nature of the business or the difficulty of appointing a suitable time or the limitation of ecclesiastical authority or anything else of the kind. They are merciless critics, who recognize only one thing in the judge's favour—deliverance from the troubles which oppress them. If he cannot offer them this, however many good reasons he gives, he will never avoid their condemnation.

And since I have already mentioned favouritism, let me disclose to you another occasion for blame. If the bishop does not pay a more extensive round of daily visits than ordinary loungers, indescribable offence will be taken. Not only the sick, but the healthy want to be visited by the bishop, not so much because their piety prompts them, as because most of them lay claim to honour and distinction. And if he happens to visit one of the richer and more influential men more frequently, prompted by some special need and for the common good of the Church, he wins at once the reputation of a flatterer and a toady.

But why mention favouritism and visiting? The mere way in which they address people is enough to incur such a load of criticism that they are often burdened and prostrated by despondency. Why, they have to render account for the

[5] I Tim. 1.19.

merest glance! People subject their casual doings to a minute examination, assessing the strength of their voice, the expression of their face, and the frequency of their laugh. "He smiled affably at so-and-so," says one, "and spoke to him with a bright face and hearty voice; but he was less pleasant with me, and indeed quite casual." When a crowd is seated together, if he does not turn his eyes in every direction while conversing, the rest say his action is an insult.

Who, then, but a man of outstanding strength could cope with so many accusers and either not be indicted by them at all, or escape after indictment? He ought to have no accusers; or if this is impossible, he should elude their accusations; and if this is not easy either, but there are some people who take pleasure in off-hand and random accusations, then he must firmly refuse to be dismayed by these complaints. A man who is justly accused can easily bear with his accuser. For since there is no accuser more bitter than our own conscience, we have no difficulty in bearing the milder accusations of others, when we have first been convicted by that most severe accuser. But when someone whose conscience acquits him of evil is accused without a cause, he is quickly roused to anger and easily falls into desperation, unless he has trained himself already to bear the mischief of the mob. For it is quite impossible for anyone who is idly slandered and accused not to be troubled and hurt by such stupid conduct. And how can one describe the grief bishops feel when anyone has to be excommunicated from the body of the Church? If only the trouble went no further than grief! But in fact it may lead to terrible loss. For it is to be feared that if a man is punished too severely, he may do what St Paul speaks of, and "be swallowed up with overmuch sorrow".[6] Here, too, great care is needed to ensure that what

[6] 2 Cor. 2.7.

was meant to help does not become the occasion of greater loss. For the vengeance for sins which he commits after such treatment is shared by the surgeon who lances the wound unskilfully.

What punishment, then, must a man expect, when he not only has to render account for his own offences but also stands in the utmost peril for the sins of others? If we shudder when our own offences are examined, for fear that we shall not be able to escape the threatened fire, what must that man expect to suffer who will have to answer for so many? To prove that this is true, hear what St Paul says, or rather, not Paul but Christ who speaks in him : "Obey them that have the rule over you and submit to them; for they watch in behalf of your souls, as they that shall give account."[7] Is the fear of this threat trivial? We dare not say it is.

Surely all this is enough to persuade the most stubborn and obstinate that my reason for hiding was not arrogance or vainglory, but fear for my own safety and a clear view of the responsibilities involved.

[7] Heb. 13.17.

11

THE PENALTY FOR FAILURE

BASIL listened to this, and after a short pause he said:

Well, if you had been personally ambitious to obtain this office. your anxiety would have been reasonable. Anyone who, by his ambition to obtain it, professes that he is suitable to exercise this ministry cannot make inexperience the excuse for his failure after he has been entrusted with it. He deprived himself of that excuse in advance, by coming forward and grabbing the ministry eagerly. And once he has voluntarily taken up the work of his own free will, he can no longer say, "I committed such and such an error against my will," or, "I did such and such a mischief against my will." For he who will judge him on that day will say: "Since you were conscious of your great inexperience and had not the ability to undertake this vocation without failure, why were you so ambitious and so presumptuous as to accept work beyond your own powers? Who compelled you to do it? Who dragged you into it forcibly, though you shied off and tried to escape?" But you, at any rate, will never hear this said to you. Nor will you have to condemn yourself for that kind of thing. It is quite clear to everyone that you never showed the least ambition for this honour, but the success of the scheme would have been due to others. What deprives the ambitious of pardon for their mistakes, provides you with good grounds for excusing yourself.

In answer to this I shook my head and smiled gently, marvelling at his simplicity, and replied:

I only wish it were as you say, my best of friends, but

not in order to enable me to accept the office which I have just evaded. For even if there were no punishment stored up for me for taking charge of the flock of Christ casually and without experience, it would be worse than any punishment to be entrusted with matters of such importance and then publicly to let down the man who had entrusted them to me.

Why, then, do I wish that your opinion were not mistaken? I do so for the sake of those wretched, miserable men (for that is what I must call those who cannot discover how to acquit themselves well in the administration of this work, however often you tell me that they were forced into it and made their mistakes in ignorance); I wish they could escape the unquenchable fire and the outer darkness and the worm that never dies and being cut asunder and perishing with the hypocrites! But what can I do? It cannot be so.

If you like, I will give you the proof of what I say, beginning with an argument from kingship, which is not so highly esteemed by God as the priesthood. When Saul, the son of Kish, was made king, he was not eager for the work. No, he set out to look for the asses and visited the prophet to inquire about them; but Samuel spoke to him about the kingship. Even then Saul did not seize it, although he had heard a prophet's words. Instead, he hesitated and excused himself, saying, "Who am I, and what is my father's house?" [1] And what happened? When he had made an evil use of the honour bestowed on him by God, did this plea suffice to save him from the anger of the one who made him king? And yet he might have answered Samuel's accusation by saying, "Did I run after the kingship? Did I rush to get this power? I wanted to live a private life in quietness and peace, but you forced me into this dignity. If I had remained

[1] Cf. 1 Sam. 9.21; 2 Sam. 7.18.

in my previous humble position, I should easily have avoided these offences; for surely if I had been one of the crowd, without special distinction, I should never have been commissioned for this work, nor would God have put me in charge of the war against the Amalekites. And if I had not been put in charge of it, I should never have committed this sin."

But all these excuses are feeble, and not only feeble but dangerous; and they rouse God's anger even more. For a man who has received an honour beyond his deserving should not use its greatness as a cloak for his faults. He ought rather to use God's abundant favour towards him as a stronger incentive to improvement. But because he has been so highly honoured, he thinks he is allowed to make mistakes, and is determined to prove that the cause of his own sins is the kindness of God. This is always the argument of irreverent men who manage their lives carelessly. We must not be like that; we must not fall into the same confusion as they do. Rather we should be at all times determined to play our part to the best of our ability, and be reverent in word and thought.

Again, to leave the kingship and come now to the priesthood, which is our real subject, Eli was not eager to obtain the office. But how did that help him when he sinned? And why do I say "obtain"? He could not have avoided it, if he had wanted to, because of the Law's demands. For he belonged to the tribe of Levi, and had to accept the hereditary office which fell to his lot in due course by reason of his birth. But even so he paid dearly for the drunken behaviour of his sons.

Then again, did not the first High Priest of the Jews, about whom God said so much to Moses, all but perish himself, except that the intercession of his brother softened God's anger, when he failed to stand alone against the madness of such a huge crowd? And since I have mentioned Moses, I might as well prove the truth of my argument from what happened to him, too. For Moses himself, of blessed memory, so far from snatching the leadership of the Jews, excused himself when it was offered to him; and although God commanded him, he continued to decline it until he roused the anger of God who appointed him. Not only then but afterwards, when he held the office, he would gladly have died to be released from it. "Kill me," he said, "if thou wilt thus deal with me." [2] What followed? When he sinned at the waters of Meribah, were his repeated refusals enough to excuse him and to persuade God to pardon him? For what else, then, was he deprived of the promised land? For nothing else, as we all know, except this sin, which was the reason why that wonderful man could not obtain the same reward as those whom he commanded. After many trials and troubles, after those incredible wanderings and wars and triumphs, he died outside the land he had struggled so hard to reach. Though he endured the hardships of the sea, he did not enjoy the blessings of the haven.

Do you see, then, that it is not only those who snatch at the office, but those who are led to it through the insistence of others, who have no excuse left when they stumble? And if those who often tried to refuse the work, but were ordained by God, were punished so severely; if nothing could save from this danger either Aaron or Eli or that blessed man, the saint, the prophet, the wonderful, who was meeker than all men on earth, who spoke as a friend with God : surely we who fall so far short of his goodness shall not be able to plead as our excuse the consciousness that we were never eager for this office—least of all in the

[2] Num. 11.15.

many cases in which these ordinations proceed, not from divine grace, but from human ambition.

God chose Judas and set him in that holy company, and granted him the rank of apostle along with the rest, and gave him something more than the rest, in the management of their money. And what happened? When he abused both of these trusts, betraying him whom he was commissioned to preach and mis-spending what he was appointed to take good care of, did he escape punishment? No, this was the very reason why he brought on himself a heavier penalty. And rightly so; for we must not misuse the honours bestowed on us by God to offend God, but to please him the more.

But a man who claims to be exempt from the punishment he deserves because he has been more highly honoured is doing much what one of the unbelieving Jews would have done if he had heard Christ say, "If I had not come and spoken unto them, they had not had sin," and, "If I had not done among them the works which none other did, they had not had sin," [3] and then had accused his Saviour and Benefactor, and said, "Why, then, did you come and speak? Why did you work miracles, so that you might punish us more severely?" Such words would be signs of madness and utter insanity. The Physician did not come to condemn you but to heal you and to rid you completely of your disease. But you wilfully refused the touch of those hands. Receive, then, heavier punishment. You would have been rid of your former diseases, if you had yielded to the treatment. But now that you have seen him coming and avoided him, you cannot any longer wash off these stains. And since you cannot, you will be punished both for them and for having frustrated his care, as much as you could.

[3] John 15.22, 24.

So we are not subjected to the same test before being honoured by God and afterwards. We have a much severer test afterwards; for if kindly treatment has not made a man good, he deserves to suffer more acutely. Since, then, I have proved that this excuse has no validity, and, so far from saving those who take refuge in it, actually betrays them to greater guilt, we must provide another safe-conduct.

Basil: What is that? For now I cannot control myself, so frightened and nervous have you made me by what you have said.

John: Do not make yourself so dejected, I beg and beseech you. There is, I assure you, a safe-conduct. For weaklings like me it is to keep clear of responsibility. For those who are strong, like you, it is to hang their hopes of salvation on nothing—after God's grace—except the avoidance of all that is unworthy of that gift and of God the giver.

The greatest punishment is deserved by men who, after getting this office by their own ambition, abuse their trust either through idleness or through wickedness or through inexperience. But I do not imply that there is any pardon, either, for those who are not ambitious for office. On the contrary, they too are stripped of all excuse. For I think that even if vast numbers of men invite and constrain you, you must not pay attention to them. First you must test your own soul, and when you have thoroughly investigated every part of it, then and then only should you give way to their constraint.

For, after all, no one who is not a builder would dare to undertake the building of a house, and no one who has not studied medicine would try to tend the bodies of the sick. On the contrary, even if a lot of people try to push them into it by force, they will excuse themselves, and not blush to confess their ignorance. And will not that man, who is to be

entrusted with the care of so many souls, first examine himself? Will he, despite his utter lack of experience, accept the
ministry because this man commands him and that man
constrains him, or for fear of offending yet another? How
can he fail to involve himself, along with them, in obvious
disaster? Left alone, he might save his own soul; but this
way he ruins others along with himself. How can he hope
for salvation? How can he find pardon? And who will intercede for us in that day? Will those perhaps who now constrain and compel us by force? But who will save them at
that hour? Truly they themselves need the help of others,
if they are to escape the fire.

To show that I do not say this to frighten you, but as the
truth of the matter is, listen to what St Paul says to his
disciple Timothy, his true and beloved child : "Lay hands
hastily on no man, neither be partaker of other men's sins."[4]
Do you see how great is the blame and the punishment from
which I have rescued, as far as I could, those who would
have brought me to this? It is not sufficient excuse for those
who have been chosen to say, "I did not come forward of my
own accord; I accepted the office with my eyes shut."
Equally, it will not help those who appoint a man to say that
they did not know the man they appointed. The fault is all
the greater because they promoted someone they did not
know. What seems to be an excuse actually increases their
guilt. Is it not peculiar that, when people want to buy a
slave, they show him to doctors and demand guarantors for
the purchase, and make inquiries of neighbours, and after
all this still lack confidence, and demand a long trial period;
yet when they are going to admit a man to this great ministry,
they make a careless and random choice without further

[4] 1 Tim. 5.22.

examination, if someone or other sees fit to vouch for him, to please or spite other people?

Who then will intercede for us at the hour when those who should stand up for us themselves need others to stand up for them? Certainly anyone who is going to confer an appointment should make a careful inquiry; but the one who is to be appointed should be more careful still. Although the people who chose him share the punishment for his sins, still he is not himself exempt from vengeance, but will pay even more dearly—unless those who chose him did so for some personal cause, against their better judgement. For if they should be detected doing so, and if they knowingly promoted the unworthy man for some unworthy reason, their punishment for presenting an unsuitable candidate will be as great as his, perhaps even greater. For if anyone gives to a man who wants to ruin the Church the power to do so, he will himself be to blame for the outrages of his nominee. But if he is innocent of all this and pleads that he has been misled by popular opinion, even then he will not escape punishment—though he will pay a rather lighter penalty than the man appointed. And why? Because it is reasonable that those who made the choice may have been deceived by a false estimate; but the man who has been chosen cannot say he did not know himself, as they can say they did not know him. Since, then, he is liable to a severer punishment than those who promoted him, he ought to make a minuter examination of his own character than they. If they bring him forward in ignorance, he should go to them and explain carefully the reasons why he must stop their being deceived. When he has shown himself unfit to survive scrutiny, he will escape the responsibility of such important work.

Why is it that when a decision has to do with war or commerce or farming or other worldly business, a farmer

would never agree to sail, nor a soldier to plough, nor a
skipper to lead an army, even if he were threatened with all
kinds of death? Obviously because each one of them foresees
the danger of inexperience. And shall we exercise such foresight and refuse to yield to compulsion, when the penalty is
trifling, but lightly and casually incur a great danger and
make the compulsion of others our excuse, when the penalty
is eternal—as it is for those who do not know how to handle
the work of the priesthood? The Judge of these matters will
not tolerate this in us on the last day. For we ought to have
shown far greater caution over spiritual than over worldly
matters. In fact, however, we are discovered exercising even
less.

Tell me, if we supposed that a man was a good craftsman
when he was no such thing, and asked him to do a job, and
he accepted; and if, when he had laid his hands on the
material provided for the building, he were to ruin the wood
and ruin the masonry and build the house in such a way
that it immediately collapsed : would it be enough excuse
for him that he was compelled to do it by others and did not
come self-invited? Certainly not. It would not be fair or
just. He ought to have kept clear of the work, even though
asked to do it by others. Shall, then, a man who ruins wood
and masonry have no refuge from justice; and shall another
who destroys souls, or builds them up carelessly, think it
enough exculpation that others compelled him? Is not that
too ingenuous? I will not add the argument that no one can
compel another against his will. Let it be granted that he
has been subjected to irresistible force and every kind of
stratagem, and so fell into the snare. Will that save him
from punishment? For goodness' sake do not let us deceive
ourselves so completely! Do not let us reply that we are
ignorant of facts which are obvious to mere children. For

surely this affectation of ignorance will not be able to help us at the Day of Judgement.

Were you reluctant to undertake this office, conscious as you were of your weakness? Very well. You should, then, on this assumption, have kept clear of it, even though others were inviting you. Were you weak and unsuitable as long as no one invited you, and did you suddenly become strong when people turned up, who would bestow the honour on you? The idea is absurd and ridiculous and deserves most severe punishment. Here is the very reason why the Lord bids the man who wants to build a tower not to lay the foundation until he has calculated his own ability, in order that he may not give those who pass by endless opportunities to poke fun at him. His penalty is no more than ridicule. But ours is fire unquenchable and the worm that never dies and gnashing of teeth and outer darkness and cutting asunder and being numbered with the hypocrites. But those who denounce us refuse to see any of this; otherwise they would have stopped blaming a man who does not want to perish all for nothing.

12

THE MINISTRY OF THE WORD

OUR PRESENT inquiry is not about dealings in wheat and barley, or oxen and sheep, or anything else of the kind. It concerns the very Body of Jesus. For the Church of Christ is Christ's own Body, according to St Paul,[1] and the man who is entrusted with it must train it to perfect health and incredible beauty, by unremitting vigilance to prevent the slightest spot or wrinkle or other blemish of that sort from marring its grace and loveliness. In short, he must make it worthy, as far as lies within human power, of that pure and blessed Head to which it is subjected.

People who are keen for athletic fitness need doctors and trainers and a careful diet and continual exercise and any amount of other precautions. For the neglect of a small detail in these matters upsets and spoils the whole scheme. Then what about those whose vocation is to look after this Body which has to contend, not against flesh and blood, but against the unseen powers? How can they keep it spotless and sound, unless they possess superhuman wisdom and fully understand the treatment suitable for the soul? Or do you not realize that that Body is liable to more diseases and attacks than this flesh of ours, and is infected more quickly and cured more slowly?

Doctors who treat the human body have discovered a multiplicity of drugs and various designs of instruments and appropriate forms of diet for the sick. And the character of the climate is often sufficient by itself to restore the patient's

[1] Col. 1.24.

health. And sometimes a timely bout of sleep relieves the doctor of all trouble. But in the present case there is nothing like this to rely on. When all is said and done, there is only one means and only one method of treatment available, and that is teaching by word of mouth. That is the best instrument, the best diet, and the best climate. It takes the place of medicine and cautery and surgery. When we need to cauterize or cut, we must use this. Without it all else is useless. By it we rouse the soul's lethargy or reduce its inflammation, we remove excrescences and supply defects, and, in short, do everything which contributes to its health.

In adopting the best possible way of life, you may be spurred on to emulation by someone else's example; but when it is false doctrine that the soul is suffering from, words are urgently needed, not only for the safety of the Church's members, but to meet the attacks of outsiders as well. If you held the sword of the Spirit and the shield of faith so firmly that you could work miracles and stop the mouths of the impudent by portents, you would have no need of the help of the word; or rather, I should say that even then the word would not be useless, but very necessary. For St Paul used it, although he aroused wonder everywhere by the signs he performed. And another of the apostolic company urges us to pay attention to this power, saying, "Be ready to give answer to every man that asketh you a reason concerning the hope that is in you." [2] Moreover, they all agreed to entrust Stephen and his fellows with the care of the widows for no other reason than that they might devote themselves to the ministry of the word. Of course, we should not be so eager for it, if we had the resource of miracles. But as there is not so much as a trace of that power left, and still many persistent enemies attack us all round, it remains

[2] 1 Pet. 3.15.

necessary for us to arm ourselves with this defence, to avoid being struck by our enemies' missiles and to strike them with ours.

We must take great care, therefore, that the word of Christ may dwell in us richly. For our preparation is not against a single kind of attack. This warfare of ours assumes complex forms and is waged by various enemies. They do not all use the same weapons and they have not all trained to attack us in the same manner. Anyone who undertakes to fight them all must know the arts of all. He must be at the same time archer and slinger, cavalry officer and infantry officer, private soldier and general, foot-soldier and hussar, marine and engineer. In military warfare each man is given a particular task and repulses the attacker in that particular way. But in our warfare this is not so. Unless the man who means to win understands every aspect of the art, the devil knows how to introduce his agents at a single neglected spot and so to plunder the flock. But he is baffled when he sees that the shepherd has mastered his whole repertoire and thoroughly understands his tricks.

So we must arm ourselves well at every point. As long as a city is encircled with walls all round, it mocks its besiegers and remains in perfect safety. But once a breach is made in the wall, no larger than a gate, the circuit is no more use to it, though all the rest stands safe. So it is with the City of God. As long as the nimble wits and the wisdom of the shepherd encompass it like a wall all round, all the enemy's devices end in his own shame and ridicule and the inhabitants remain unharmed; but when someone manages to break down a part of this defence, even though he fails to destroy it all, from that moment practically the whole city is ruined through that one part. What if the Jews pillage the Church while it is contending successfully against the

Greeks? or if it masters both of these, but is plundered by the Manichaeans? or if, after it has overcome these too, the exponents of "Destiny" [3] slaughter the sheep standing inside the fold? Do I need to enumerate all the devil's heresies? But unless the shepherd knows how to refuse every one of them effectively, the wolf can enter by a single one and devour most of the sheep.

In the case of soldiers, we must always expect that victory or defeat will depend on those who stand and fight. But in our case it is far different. Often the battle against others secures victory for men who did not enter the fight or endure its toil at all, but were sitting still and doing nothing. And if someone falls on his own sword through lack of wide experience in these conflicts, he becomes an object of ridicule to friend and foe alike.

I shall try to explain my meaning to you by an example. Those who accept the nonsense taught by Valentinus and Marcion, and all who are infected with their disease, reject the Law given by God to Moses from the canon of Holy Scripture. The Jews, on the other hand, hold it in such reverence that they obstinately try to observe it all, contrary to God's will, though circumstances prevent them. But the Church of God, avoiding both extremes, steers a middle course, and neither lets herself be subjected to its yoke nor permits men to disparage it, but commends it, although it is abrogated, because it was serviceable in its time. So anyone who means to oppose both these parties must understand this balance. If he wants to teach the Jews that they are out of date in clinging to their ancient legislation, and begins to disparage it unsparingly, he gives an easy handle to those heretics who want to tear it in pieces. But if, in his determination to silence this group, he extols the Law immoder-

[3] The Stoics, against whom John Chrysostom wrote six homilies.

ately and admires it as though it were necessary in our present age, he opens the mouths of the Jews.

Again, those who are afflicted with the madness of Sabellius or the ravings of Arius have in both cases fallen away from the sound faith by going to extremes. Each of these parties bears the name of Christian, but if you examine their doctrines you will find the first group no better than Jews except for a difference of name, while the others have a great affinity with the heresy of Paul of Samosata; and both are beyond the pale of truth. There is, then, great danger in such cases, and strait and narrow is the way, with abrupt precipices on both sides. There is every reason to fear that, while trying to aim a blow at one enemy, you will be struck by the other. If someone says that the Godhead is one, Sabellius distorts the expression at once, to favour his own madness. If, on the other hand, someone makes a distinction and says that the Father is one, the Son another, and the Holy Ghost another, up gets Arius, twisting the distinction of Persons into a difference of Substance. We must shun and avoid the impious confusion of the one party and the mad division of the other by confessing that the Godhead of the Father and the Son and the Holy Ghost is one, but adding that there are three Persons. For by this means we shall be able to defend ourselves from the attacks of both.

I could tell you of many other struggles from which it will cost you a great many scars to extricate yourself, unless you fight with courage and with care. Need I mention the idle speculations of our own people? They are quite as many as the attacks from outside, and they cause the teacher even more trouble. Some people, out of restless curiosity, want to elaborate idly and irresponsibly doctrines which are of no benefit to those who understand them, or else are actually

incomprehensible. Others call God to account for his judgements and struggle to measure the great deep. For the
Psalmist says : "Thy judgements are a great deep."[4] You
will find that few are deeply concerned about faith and conduct, but the majority go in for these elaborate theories and
investigate questions to which there is no answer and whose
very investigation rouses God's anger. For when we struggle
to learn things which God himself did not will us to know,
we shall never succeed—how can we, against God's will?—
and we shall gain nothing but our own peril from the investigation.

But, for all that, when anyone uses authority to silence
people who pursue these enigmas, he gets a reputation for
arrogance and ignorance. So here, too, the president needs
great tact to dissuade men from inappropriate speculations
and to escape the criticisms I have mentioned. For all these
matters no other help has been vouchsafed but that of the
word. And if anyone is deprived of this power, the souls of
those under him (I mean the weaker and more speculative of
them) will be not better off than ships storm-tossed at sea. So
the priest should do all he can to gain this power.

Basil: Why then was not Paul eager to attain perfection
in this quality? He is not ashamed of his poverty of speech,
but expressly confesses that he is inexpert at it.[5] And he says
this when writing to the Corinthians who were admired for
their eloquence and prided themselves on it.

John: This is the very excuse that has ruined most men
and made them more casual about true doctrine. Being
unable to examine with care the profundity of the Apostle's
mind or to understand the meaning of his words, they have
spent all their time nodding and yawning, and prizing, not

<hr>

[4] Ps. 36.6.   [5] 2 Cor. 11.6.

the form of ignorance which Paul admitted, but a form from which no man under heaven was ever as free.

But let the statement stand for the moment. In the meantime I say this : let us assume that he was inexpert in this faculty, as they maintain; what has that to do with the present argument? He had a greater power than speech, a power which was able to effect greater results. By his mere presence, and without a word, he terrified the devils. If the men of to-day were all to join forces, they could not with any quantity of prayers and tears do as much as the handkerchiefs of Paul once did. Paul by his prayers used to raise the dead and work miracles so wonderful that he was regarded as a god by the heathen. And before he departed this life he was thought worthy to be caught up to the third heaven and to listen to words which are not lawful for human kind to hear. But as for the men of to-day—and I do not want to say anything unkind or severe; no indeed, for I am not speaking to reproach them, but only in amazement—how can they avoid shuddering when they compare themselves with so great a man? For if we pass over his miracles and come to the saint's life and examine his angelic behaviour, we shall see the Christian athlete a conqueror here even more than in his miracles. Need I mention his earnestness, his forbearance, his continual perils, his constant cares, his unceasing anxieties for the churches, his sympathy with the weak, his many tribulations, his unexampled persecutions, his daily deaths? What place in the world, what continent or sea remained ignorant of the struggles of that just man? Even the desert knew him and sheltered him often when he was in peril. He endured every form of intrigue. He won every kind of victory. His efforts never ceased, nor ceased being crowned.

But I do not know how I let myself insult him. For his

achievements surpass all description; they certainly surpass my description as much as practised orators surpass me. Yet since the saint will not judge me by results but by intentions, I will not stop until I have stated one fact which is as much above what I have said as he is above all other men. And what is that? After all these achievements, after winning laurels past number, he prayed that he might go to hell and be delivered to eternal punishment, to bring it about that the Jews, who had often stoned him and done what they could to murder him, might be saved and come to Christ. Who longed for Christ as he did?—if indeed we may call it longing and not by some stronger name. Shall we, then, continue to compare ourselves with him, when we recall the great grace which he received from above and the great virtue which he displayed in himself? What could be more presumptuous than that!

And now I will try to prove also that, despite all this, he was not inexpert at speaking, in the way that these men think. For they do not apply the title merely to one who is unversed in the pedantry of heathen rhetoric, but also to one who does not understand how to contend for the doctrines of the Truth. And they are right. But Paul did not say he was inexpert at both these qualities; only the former. To establish this fact he carefully made the distinction by saying that he was "inexpert in speech, but not in knowledge". Now if I were demanding the polish of Isocrates and the grandeur of Demosthenes and the dignity of Thucydides and the sublimity of Plato, it would be right to confront me with the testimony of Paul. But in fact I pass over all those qualities and the superfluous embellishments of pagan writers. I take no account of diction or style. Let a man's diction be beggarly and his verbal composition simple and artless, but do not let him be inexpert in the knowledge and careful statement of doctrine. And do not let him deprive the saint, to cloak his own idleness, of the greatest of his qualities and the chief of his claims of eulogy.

Tell me, how did he confound the Jews dwelling in Damascus, when he had not yet begun his miracles? How did he confute the Grecians? Why was he sent to Tarsus? Was it not because he powerfully prevailed by his words and so far routed them that they were provoked to murder him, not being able to bear their defeat? Then he had not yet begun to work wonders and no one could say that the crowds thought him wonderful because of the fame of his miracles or that the people who opposed him were overthrown by his reputation. For at that time his only power was the power of speech. How did he contend and dispute with those who tried to live like Jews at Antioch?[6] Did not the Areopagite, who belonged to that very superstitious city,[7] follow him with his wife because of his speech alone? How did Eutychus come to fall from the window? Was it not because he was engrossed until midnight in the word of his teaching? What happened at Thessalonica and Corinth? What at Ephesus and Rome itself? Did he not spend whole days and nights continuously in expounding the Scriptures? Need we mention his disputes with the Epicureans and Stoics? If I wanted to tell all, my account would stretch to an excessive length. But when he obviously made much use of argument, both before he began his miracles and after he had begun them, how can anyone dare to call him inexpert at speaking—the man who won everyone's admiration above all by his disputations and public speeches? Why did the Lycaonians believe him to be Hermes? The idea that he and Barnabas were gods was due to their miracles; but the idea

[6] Gal. 2.11 ff.   [7] Acts 17.34.

that he was Hermes was due not to his miracles but to his eloquence.

In what did St Paul surpass the rest of the Apostles? And how does it come about that throughout the whole world he is much on everyone's lips? How is it that, not merely among ourselves, but among Jews and Greeks too, he is admired beyond all men? Is it not because of the excellence of his Epistles? By this he has helped and will help and, as long as the human race remains, will never stop helping the faithful, not only of his own time but from that day to this and those who shall believe until the coming of Christ. For his writings fortify the churches all over the world like a wall of steel. Even now he stands among us like some noble champion, bringing into captivity every thought to the obedience of Christ and casting down imaginations and every high thing that is exalted against the knowledge of God. All this he does by means of those wonderful Epistles he has left us, so full of divine wisdom.

His writings are not only useful to us for the refutation of false doctrine and the establishment of the true, but they help us very greatly, too, in living a good life. For by the use of them even to-day the presidents educate and train the pure Virgin whom Paul himself espoused to Christ, and lead her on to spiritual beauty. By them they also ward off the diseases which attack her, and preserve the good health she enjoys. Such is the quality and such the strength of the medicines left us by this man who was inexpert at speaking! Those who use them constantly know their worth.

These facts are enough to show that he took great pains over this part of his work. But listen also to what he says to his disciple in a letter: "Give heed to reading, to exhortation, to teaching."[8] And he adds the fruit which develops

[8] I Tim. 4.13.

from this : "For in doing this," he says, "thou shalt save both thyself and them that hear thee"; and again, "And the Lord's servant must not strive, but be gentle towards all, apt to teach, forbearing."[9] And further on he says, "But abide thou in the things which thou hast learned and hast been assured of, knowing of whom thou has learned them; and that from a babe thou hast known the sacred writings which are able to make thee wise";[10] and again, "Every scripture inspired of God is also profitable for teaching, for reproof, for correction, for instruction which is in righteousness : that the man of God may be complete."[11] And listen to what he adds in his charge to Titus about the appointment of bishops : "For the bishop," he says, "must hold to the faithful word which is according to the teaching, that he may be able to convict even the gainsayers."[12] How, then, if he is inexpert at speaking, as they say, will he be able to convict the gainsayers and to stop their mouths? And why need anyone give heed to reading and to the scriptures, if it is right to welcome such inexpertness? This is all just a pretence and excuse and a pretext for carelessness and indolence.

Basil: But this charge is given to the priests.

John: Well, our argument just now is about priests. But to learn that he gives it also to those who are under authority, listen to some advice he gives to others in another epistle : "Let the word of Christ dwell in you richly in all wisdom";[13] and again, "Let your speech be always with grace, seasoned with salt, that ye may know how ye ought to answer each one".[14] And the command to be ready to give an answer[15] was given to all alike. Writing to the Thessalonians, Paul

---

[9] 2 Tim. 2.24.   [10] 2 Tim. 3.14–15.   [11] 2 Tim. 3.16–17.
[12] Titus 1.7–9.   [13] Col. 3.16.   [14] Col. 4.6.
                        [15] 1 Pet. 3.15.

says, "Build each other up, even as also ye do."[16] But when he speaks of priests, he says, "Let the elders that rule well be counted worthy of double honour, especially those who labour in the word and in teaching."[17] For this is the ultimate aim of their teaching : to lead their disciples, both by what they do and what they say, into the way of that blessed life which Christ commanded. Example alone is not sufficient instruction. And this statement is not mine, but the Saviour's own. For he says, 'Whosoever shall do and teach, he shall be called great."[18] Now if to do were the same as to teach, the second word would be superfluous. It would have been enough to say "Whosoever shall do." But in fact by distinguishing the two he shows that example is one thing and instruction another, and that each requires the other for perfect edification.

Do you recall what the chosen vessel[19] of Christ said to the elders of Ephesus? "Wherefore, watch ye, remembering that by the space of three years I ceased not to admonish every one of you night and day with tears."[20] What need was there of tears or of verbal admonition, when the Apostle's life shone so bright? For the keeping of the commandments his holy life might be a great help to us—though even here I should not say that example alone could achieve everything. But when conflict arises on matters of doctrine and all the combatants rely on the same scriptures, what weight will his life carry then? What use are a man's many labours, when after all his exertions he falls into heresy through sheer inexperience and is cut off from the body of the Church, as I know many have done? What help is his perseverance? None at all—no more, in fact, than a sound faith coupled with a corrupt life. That is the chief reason why anyone who

[16] I Thess. 5.11.   [17] I Tim. 5.17.   [18] Matt. 5.19.
[19] Cf. Acts 9.15.   [20] Acts 20.31.

has the responsibility of teaching others must be experienced in these doctrinal conflicts. For though he himself stands secure and is not injured by his opponents; yet, when the multitude of simpler folk who are set under him see their leader worsted and unable to answer his opponents, they do not blame his incapacity for the defeat, but his unsound doctrine. So through the inexperience of one man the whole congregation is brought to ultimate disaster. Though they may not quite join the enemy, yet they cannot help doubting, where they used to be confident. Those whom they used to consult with unwavering faith they can no longer attend to with the same security. Such a storm invades their souls because of their teacher's defeat that the evil leads at last to shipwreck. What awful disaster, what burning fire is heaped on that wretched man's head for every one of these souls that perish, you do not need me to tell you, since you know it all perfectly well.

Is it, then, due to arrogance, is it due to vainglory, if I refused to be the cause of perdition to so many and to earn for myself a severer punishment than that which now awaits me in the world to come? Who could say so? No one, unless he wanted to cast idle aspersions and speculate upon another's misfortunes.

13

TEMPTATIONS OF THE TEACHER

I HAVE given sufficient proof of the experience needed by the teacher in contending for the truth. I have one thing more to add to this, a cause of untold dangers : or rather, I will not blame the thing itself so much as those who do not know how to use it properly; in itself it conduces to salvation and to many benefits, when it happens to be handled by earnest, good men. And what is it? It is the great toil expended upon sermons delivered publicly to the congregation.

In the first place, most of those who are under authority refuse to treat preachers as their instructors. They rise above the status of disciples and assume that of spectators sitting in judgement on secular speech-making. In their case the audience is divided, and some side with one speaker and others side with another. So in church they divide and become partisans, some of this preacher and some of that, listening to their words with favour or dislike. And this is not the only difficulty; there is another, no less serious. If it happens that a preacher weaves among his own words a proportion of other men's flowers, he falls into worse disgrace than a common thief. And often when he has borrowed nothing at all, he suffers on bare suspicion the fate of a convicted felon. But why mention the work of others? He is not allowed to repeat his own compositions too soon. For most people usually listen to a preacher for pleasure, not profit, like adjudicators of a play or concert. The power of eloquence, which we rejected just now, is more requisite in a church than when professors of rhetoric are made to contend against each other !

Here, too, a man needs a loftiness of mind far beyond my own littleness of spirit, if he is to correct this disorderly and unprofitable delight of ordinary people, and to divert their attention to something more useful, so that church people will follow and defer to him and not that he will be governed by their desires. It is impossible to acquire this power except by these two qualities : contempt of praise and the force of eloquence. If either is lacking, the one left is made useless through divorce from the other. If a preacher despises praise, yet does not produce the kind of teaching which is "with grace, seasoned with salt",[1] he is despised by the people and gets no advantage from his sublimity. And if he manages this side of things perfectly well, but is a slave to the sound of applause, again an equal damage threatens both him and the people, because through his passion for praise he aims to speak more for the pleasure than the profit of his hearers. The man who is unaffected by acclamation, yet unskilled in preaching, does not truckle to the people's pleasure; but no more can he confer any real benefit upon them, because he has nothing to say. And equally, the man who is carried away with the desire for eulogies may have the ability to improve the people, but chooses instead to provide nothing but entertainment. That is the price he pays for thunders of applause.

The perfect ruler, then, must be strong in both points, to stop one being nullified by the other. When he stands up in the congregation and says things capable of stinging the careless, the good done by what he has said leaks away quickly if he then stumbles and stops and has to blush for want of words. Those who stand rebuked, being nettled by his words and unable to retaliate on him in any other way, jeer at him for his lack of skill, thinking to mask their shame

[1] Col. 4.6.

by doing so. So, like a good charioteer, the preacher should have reached perfection in both these qualities, in order to be able to handle both of them as need requires. For only when he is himself beyond reproach in everyone's eyes will he be able, with all the authority he desires, to punish or pardon all who are in his charge. But until then it will not be easy to do.

But this sublimity must not only be displayed in contempt for applause; it must go further, if its benefit is not in turn to be wasted. What else, then, must he despise? Slander and envy. The right course is neither to show disproportionate fear and anxiety over ill-directed abuse (for the president will have to put up with unfounded criticism), nor simply to ignore it. We should try to extinguish criticisms at once, even if they are false and are levelled at us by quite ordinary people. For nothing will magnify a good or evil report as much as an undisciplined crowd. Being accustomed to hear and speak uncritically, they give hasty utterance to whatever occurs to them, without any regard for the truth. So we must not disregard the multitude, but rather nip their evil suspicions in the bud by convincing our accusers, however unreasonable they may be. We should leave nothing untried that might destroy an evil report. But if, when we have done all, our critics will not be convinced, then at last we must resort to contempt. For anyone who goes half-way to meet humiliation by things like this will never be able to achieve anything fine or admirable. For despondency and constant anxieties have a terrible power to numb the soul and reduce it to utter impotence.

The priest should treat those whom he rules as a father treats very young children. We are not disturbed by children's insults or blows or tears; nor do we think much of their laughter and approval. And so with these people, we

should not be much elated by their praise nor much dejected
by their censure, when we get these things from them out of
season. This is not easy, my friend, and I think it may be
impossible. I do not know whether anyone has ever succeeded in not enjoying praise. If he enjoys it, he naturally
wants to receive it. And if he wants to receive it, he cannot
help being pained and distraught at losing it. People who
enjoy being wealthy take it hard when they fall into poverty,
and those who are used to luxury cannot bear to live
frugally. So, too, men who are in love with applause have
their spirits starved not only when they are blamed off-hand,
but even when they fail to be constantly praised. Especially
is this so when they have been brought up on applause, or
when they hear others being praised.

What troubles and vexations do you suppose a man en-
dures, if he enters the lists of preaching with this ambition
for applause? The sea can never be free from waves; no
more can his soul be free from cares and sorrow. For though
a man may have great force as a speaker (which you will
rarely find), still he is not excused continual effort. For the
art of speaking comes, not by nature, but by instruction, and
therefore even if a man reaches the acme of perfection in it,
still it may forsake him unless he cultivates its force by
constant application and exercise. So the gifted have even
harder work than the unskilful. For the penalty for neglect
is not the same for both, but varies in proportion to their
attainments. No one would blame the unskilful for turning
out nothing remarkable. But gifted speakers are pursued by
frequent complaints from all and sundry, unless they continually surpass the expectation which everyone has of them.
Besides this, the unskilful can win great praise for small
successes, but as for the others, unless their efforts are very

startling and stupendous, they not only forfeit all praise, but have a host of carping critics.

For the congregation does not sit in judgement on the sermon as much as on the reputation of the preacher, so that when someone excels everyone else at speaking, then he above all needs painstaking care. He is not allowed sometimes not to succeed—the common experience of all the rest of humanity. On the contrary, unless his sermons always match the great expectations formed of him, he will leave the pulpit the victim of countless jeers and complaints. No one ever takes it into consideration that a fit of depression, pain, anxiety, or in many cases anger, may cloud the clarity of his mind and prevent his productions from coming forth unalloyed; and that in short, being a man, he cannot invariably reach the same standard or always be successful, but will naturally make many mistakes and obviously fall below the standard of his real ability. People are unwilling to allow for any of these factors, as I said, but criticize him as if they were sitting in judgement on an angel. And anyhow men are so made that they overlook their neighbour's successes, however many or great; yet if a defect comes to light, however commonplace and however long since it last occurred, it is quickly noticed, fastened on at once, and never forgotten. So a trifling and unimportant fault has often curtailed the glory of many fine achievements.

You see, my dear fellow, that the ablest speaker has all the more need for careful application, and not application only, but greater tolerance than any of those I have so far mentioned. For plenty of people keep attacking him without rhyme or reason. They hate him without having anything against him except his universal popularity. And he must put up with their acrimonious envy with composure. For since they do not cover up and hide this accursed hatred which they entertain without reason, they shower him with abuse and complaints and secret slander and open malice. And the soul which begins by feeling pain and annoyance about each of these things cannot avoid being desolated with grief. For they not only attack him by their own efforts, but they set about doing so through others as well. They often choose someone who has no speaking ability and cry him up with their praises and admire him quite beyond his deserts. Some do this through sheer ignorance and others through ignorance and envy combined, to ruin the good speaker's reputation, not to win admiration for one who does not deserve it.

And that high-minded man has to contend, not just against this kind of opponent, but often against the ignorance of a whole community. For it is impossible for a whole congregation to be made up of men of distinction; and it generally happens that the greater part of the Church consists of ignorant people. The rest are perhaps superior to these, but fall short of men of critical ability by a wider margin than the great majority fall short of them. Scarcely one or two present have acquired real discrimination. And so it is inevitable that the more capable speaker receives less applause and sometimes even goes away without any mark of approval. He must face these ups and downs in a noble spirit, pardoning those whose opinion is due to ignorance, grieving over those who maintain an attitude out of envy, as miserable, pitiable creatures, and letting neither make him think the less of his powers. For if a painter of first rank who excelled all others in skill, saw the picture he had painted with great care scoffed at by men ignorant of art, he ought not to be dejected or to regard his painting as poor, because of the judgement of the ignorant; just as little should he regard a really poor work as wonderful and charming because the unlearned admired it.

Let the best craftsman be the judge of his own handiwork too, and let us rate his productions as beautiful or poor when that is the verdict of the mind which contrived them. But as for the erratic and unskilled opinion of outsiders, we should not so much as consider it. So too the man who has accepted the task of teaching should pay no attention to the commendation of outsiders, any more than he should let them cause him dejection. When he has composed his sermons to please God (and let this alone be his rule and standard of good oratory in sermons, not applause or commendation), then if he should be approved by men too, let him not spurn their praise. But if his hearers do not accord it, let him neither seek it or sorrow for it. It will be sufficient encouragement for his efforts, and one much better than anything else, if his conscience tells him that he is organizing and regulating his teaching to please God. For in fact, if he has already been overtaken by the desire for unmerited praise, neither his great efforts nor his powers of speech will be any use. His soul, being unable to bear the senseless criticisms of the multitude, grows slack and loses all earnestness about preaching. So a preacher must train himself above all else to despise praise. For without this addition, knowledge of the technique of speaking is not enough to ensure powerful speech.

And even if you choose to investigate carefully the type of man who lacks this gift of eloquence, you will find he needs to despise praise just as much as the other type. For he will inevitably make many mistakes, if he lets himself be dominated by popular opinion. Being incapable of matching popular preachers in point of eloquence, he will not hesitate to plot against them, to envy them, to criticize them idly, and to do a lot of other disgraceful things. He will dare anything, if it costs him his very soul, to bring their reputation down to the level of his own insignificance. Besides this, he will give up the sweat of hard work, because a kind of numbness has stolen over his spirit. For it is enough to dispirit a man who cannot disdain praise and reduce him to a deep lethargy, when he toils hard but earns all the less approbation. When a farmer labours on poor land and is forced to farm a rocky plot, he soon gives up his toil, unless he is full of enthusiasm for his work, or is driven on by fear of starvation.

If those who can preach with great force need such constant practice to preserve their gift, what about someone who has absolutely no reserves in hand, but needs to get preaching practice by actually preaching? How much difficulty and mental turmoil and trouble must he put up with, to be able to build up his resources just a little by a lot of labour! And if any of his colleagues of inferior rank can excel him in this particular work, he really needs to be divinely inspired to avoid being seized with envy or thrown into dejection. It requires no ordinary character (and certainly not one like mine) but one of steel, for a man who holds a superior position to be excelled by his inferiors and to bear it with dignity. If the man who outstrips him in reputation is unassuming and very modest, the experience is just tolerable. But if he is impudent and boastful and vainglorious, his superior may as well pray daily to die, so unpleasant will the other man make his life by flouting him to his face and mocking him behind his back, by detracting frequently from his authority and aiming to be everything himself. And his rival will have derived great assurance in all this from the licence people grant him to say what he likes, the warm interest of the majority in him, and the affection of those under his charge. Or do you not know what a passion for oratory has recently infatuated Christians? Do you not know that its exponents are respected above everyone else, not just by outsiders, but by those of the household of faith? How, then, can anyone endure the deep disgrace of having his sermon received with blank silence and feelings of boredom, and his listeners waiting for the end of the sermon as if it were a relief after fatigue; whereas they listen to someone else's sermon, however long, with eagerness, and are annoyed when he is about to finish and quite exasperated when he decides to say no more?

Perhaps this seems to you a trifling, negligible matter, because you have no experience of it. Yet it is enough to kill enthusiasm and paralyse spiritual energy, unless a man dispossesses himself of all human passions and studies to live like the disembodied spirits who are not hounded by envy or vainglory or any other disease of that sort. If there actually is anyone capable of subduing this elusive, invincible, savage monster (I mean popular esteem) and cutting off its many heads, or rather, preventing their growth altogether, he will be able to repulse all these attacks easily and enjoy a quiet haven of rest. But if he has not shaken himself free of it, he involves his soul in an intricate struggle, in unrelieved turmoil, and in the hurly-burly of desperation and every other passion. Why should I catalogue all the other troubles, which no one can describe or realize without personal experience?

14

THE NEED FOR PURITY

So much, then, for this world. But how shall we fare in the world to come when we are made to account for every single one committed to our charge? Then the penalty will not be just disgrace; eternal punishment awaits us. I cannot help quoting here the passage I have already mentioned : "Obey them that have the rule over you and submit to them; for they watch in behalf of your souls, as they that shall give account."[1] The fear of this threat continually disturbs my spirit. If it is better for a man who offends just one other person, and him the least of all, that a millstone should be hanged about his neck and that he should be sunk in the depth of the sea;[2] and if all who wound the conscience of the brethren, sin against Christ himself :[3] what will be the fate and what the punishment of those who ruin, not one or two or three, but great multitudes? They cannot even plead inexperience, or take refuge in a plea of ignorance or make force and constraint their excuse. It would be more suitable for someone under authority to use this excuse for his own sins, if possible, than for their rulers to use it in the case of other people's sins. And why? Because the man whose responsibility it is to rectify the ignorance of the rest and to give warning when conflict with the devil is approaching will not be able to make ignorance his excuse or say, "I did not hear the clarion", or "I did not know the conflict was coming". For as Ezekiel says, he is appointed for this very purpose, to sound the alarm for the rest and give warning

[1] Heb. 13.17.   [2] Matt. 18.6.   [3] 1 Cor. 8.12.

of trouble ahead.[4] And so his punishment is inexorable, even
if the casualties are no more than one. "For if the watchman
see the sword come," says Ezekiel, "and blow not the
trumpet nor warn the people, and the sword come and take
any person; he indeed is taken away for his iniquity, but his
blood will I require at the watchman's hand."[5]

Stop pushing me, then, towards such inevitable punishment. For we are not discussing military command or kingship, but something that requires angelic virtue. For the
priest's soul must be purer than the rays of the sun, in order
that the Holy Spirit may never leave him desolate, and that
he may be able to say, "I live; yet no longer I, but Christ
liveth in me".[6]

Even hermits living in the desert, far away from city and
market-place and the distractions they cause, although they
continually enjoy a haven and a calm sea, are unwilling to
rely on the security of that way of life, but add innumerable
other safeguards, and hedge themselves in all round. They
take care to be very precise in all they say and do, on purpose to be able to approach God with frankness and with
spotless purity, as far as a man can do so. How much ability,
then, and how much strength do you suppose the priest
needs to enable him to keep his soul from every contamina-
tion and preserve its spiritual beauty unimpaired? He needs
far greater purity than they do. And since he has the greater
need, he is a prey to more temptations, which can defile him
unless he makes his soul inaccessible to them by the practice
of unremitting self-denial and strict self-discipline. There is
enough to upset his spirit—unless it is desiccated by the
very exacting demands of self-control—in pretty faces,
affected movements, a mincing walk, a silvery voice, eyes
dark with shadow, painted cheeks, complicated hair styles,

[4] Ezek. 3.17.   [5] Cf. Ezek. 33.6.   [6] Gal. 2.20.

tinted hair, expensive clothes, gold ornaments in plenty, fine
jewellery, sweet perfumes, and all the other tricks of womankind.

It is not surprising that a man should be distracted by
things like these. What is thoroughly strange and bewilder-
ing is that the devil should be able to hit and shoot down
the souls of men by the very opposites of these, too! Before
now some men who have escaped these traps, have been
caught in others quite different. Even a neglected appear-
ance, unkempt hair, slovenly clothing, absence of make-up,
simple behaviour, artless language, an unstudied gait, a
natural voice, a life of poverty, and a despised, unprotected,
and lonely existence, have led the beholder first to com-
passion and then to utter downfall. Many who have escaped
the first kind of snare, consisting of gold ornaments, perfume,
and clothing, and the other things I mentioned, have been
easily trapped by these very different things, and have gone
to perdition.

Both by penury and wealth, both by the use of make-up
and a neglected look, both by affected and by natural man-
ners, in short, by all the means I have enumerated, turmoil
is aroused in the mind of the beholder and the engines of
war beset him all round. So where will he get a respite, with
so many snares encircling him? What hiding-place can he
find, I do not say just to avoid being forcibly captured (for
that is not so very difficult), but to keep his own mind un-
troubled by defiling thoughts?

I pass over honours, which give rise to a host of evils.
Those bestowed by women damage the sinews of self-
restraint and often destroy them altogether, when a man
does not know how to keep continual watch against such
insidious temptations. As for the honours bestowed by men,
unless anyone receives them with great dignity, he is trapped

by two contrary feelings, by the servile spirit of toadyism and by the insanity of boastfulness. He is forced to be subservient to those who patronize him and he behaves conceitedly towards humbler brethren because of honours bestowed by his patrons, and is thrust into the pit of arrogance.

I have simply mentioned these matters; but no one could properly learn how much harm they do, without actual experience. For not only these temptations but others too, far more numerous and far more perilous than these, inevitably attack men who lead their lives in the thick of things. Anyone who loves solitude has immunity from all this; or if ever a depraved imagination suggests some such idea to him, the mental picture is faint and easily suppressed, because there is no extra fuel for the flame supplied by sight from the external world. And then the monk fears for himself alone; or if he is compelled to take responsibility for others, they are very few; or if they are many, still they are fewer than those in the churches and cause their superintendent far lighter worries about them, not only because their numbers are small, but also because they are all free from worldly business and have no need to concern themselves about children or anything else of the kind. This makes them very obedient to their rulers and leads them to share a common dwelling, so that someone can carefully watch and correct their failings; and this fact—the constant supervision of a master—contributes considerably to their virtue. But most of those who are subject to the priest are shackled with worldly cares, and this makes them more sluggish in the discharge of spiritual duties. Therefore the master must sow his seed practically every day, so that through sheer repetition the word of teaching may be held fast by those who hear. For excessive wealth, great power,

indolence arising from luxury, and many other things choke
the seeds that are sown. Often the thick growth of thorns
does not allow what is sown to fall even as far as the surface
of the soil. And again, often the very opposite of these—too
much distress, the pinch of poverty, continual insults, and
other troubles of that sort—abate men's concern for the
things of God. And not even a fraction of their sins can be
known to the priests. How could it be otherwise, when they
do not know the majority even by sight?

Such are the difficulties of their duties towards the people.
But if you go into their duty to God, you will find these
difficulties as nothing, since so much greater and more
painstaking care is required for this. What sort of man
ought someone to be, who is an ambassador for a whole city
—no, not just a city : the whole world—and begs God to be
merciful to the sins of all men, not only the living, but the
departed too? I do not think that even the confidence of a
Moses or Elijah is adequate for this great intercession. He
approaches God as if he were responsible for the whole
world, and himself the father of all men, praying that wars
everywhere may end and tumults cease, supplicating for
peace and prosperity, and a speedy release from all ills,
private or public, that threaten any man. He must so far
surpass all those for whom he intercedes in all qualities as
one in authority ought properly to surpass those under his
charge. But when he invokes the Holy Spirit and offers that
awful sacrifice and keeps on touching the common Master
of us all, tell me, where shall we rank him? What purity and
what piety shall we demand of him? Consider how spotless
should the hands be that administer these things, how holy
the tongue that utters these words. Ought anyone to have a
purer and holier soul than one who is to welcome this great
Spirit? At that moment angels attend the priest, and the

whole dais and the sanctuary are thronged with heavenly powers in honour of Him who lies there.

The actual rites which are performed at that moment are enough to demonstrate this. But I have also heard someone relate the following story. An old, venerable man, who was accustomed to see visions, told him that he had been privileged actually to see it. At that very moment he had suddenly seen, to the extent of his ability, a host of angels clad in bright robes, encircling the altar and bowing their heads, as you would see soldiers bow, when standing in the presence of their king. Personally, I believe the story. And someone else told me, not from hearsay but as one who had been permitted to see and hear it, that when men are about to pass away, if they happen to have received the Mysteries with a pure conscience just before they breathe their last, a bodyguard of angels escorts them away for the sake of what they have received.

Are you not yet frightened at bringing a spirit like mine to such solemn consecration and promoting to the priestly dignity the man wearing dirty clothes whom Christ himself expelled from the general company of guests?[7] The soul of the priest ought to blaze like a light illuminating the world; but my soul has such darkness enveloping it, through my evil conscience, that it is always hiding itself and cannot frankly gaze upon its Master. Priests are the salt of the earth. But who could readily tolerate my folly and my complete inexperience, except you with your usual excessive regard for me? A priest must not only be blameless, as befits one chosen for so high a ministry, but also very discreet and widely experienced. He ought to be as much aware of mundane matters as any who live in the midst of them, and yet

[7] Matt. 22.11.

be more detached from them than the monks who have taken to the mountains.

Since he must mix with men who have married and are bringing up children, keep servants, own great possessions, take part in public life, and hold high office, he must be many-sided. I say many-sided—not a charlatan, a flatterer, or a hypocrite; but absolutely open and frank of speech, able to condescend to good purpose, when the situation requires, and to be alike kindly or severe. It is impossible to treat all his people in one way, any more than it would be right for the doctors to deal with all their patients alike or a helmsman to know only one way of battling with the winds. This ship of ours is beset with continual storms; and these storms not only attack from outside, but are engendered within. Great condescension and great strictness are both needed. And all these different methods look to one object : the glory of God and the edification of the Church.

15

THE CONTRAST BETWEEN BISHOP
AND MONK

THE MONKS' exertion is great and the strain severe; but if you compare their labours with the priestly office, when properly exercised, you will find the difference is as great as between a private citizen and a king. In their case, although the task is hard, still the conflict is shared between soul and body; or rather, it is chiefly carried to success by a system of bodily exercises. And if the body is not strong, enthusiasm remains pent up, having no outlet in practice; for it is obvious that prolonged fasting, sleeping on the ground, vigils, abstention from washing, hard labour, and all other exercises which tend towards the mortification of the flesh, are impossible if the intending ascetic is not strong. But in the case we are considering, the skill is purely one of the spirit, and no bodily vigour is needed besides, to show its excellence. How does bodily strength help us not to be stubborn or hot-tempered or reckless, but sober, prudent, and orderly, and everything else with which St Paul filled out the picture of the perfect priest? Yet no one could say this of the qualities proper to a monk.

As jugglers need a lot of implements—wheels, ropes, and daggers—but the philosopher has his entire art stored in his soul and needs nothing from outside; so in our case, the monk needs a good bodily constitution, and a place suitable to his method of life, in order that he may not be too far from human society and yet may enjoy the quiet of solitude, and may not miss the most suitable climate; for nothing is so hard to bear, for one worn with fasting, as an inequable climate. I need not mention here how much trouble over the provision of clothing and food he is bound to have, since he has set himself the aim of entire self-sufficiency. But the priest will require none of these things for his own use. He avoids needless difficulties, shares in all innocent occupations, and holds all his skill stored up in the treasuries of his soul.

If anyone admires a solitary life and the avoidance of crowded society, I quite admit that it is a paradigm of patient endurance, but not sufficient proof of all-round spiritual prowess. In harbour the man at the helm cannot yet give sure proof of his skill; but no one will deny the title of a first-class helmsman to anyone who guides his ship to safety in the midst of a stormy sea. We need not, then, give lavish or excessive admiration to the monk because, by keeping himself to himself, he avoids agitation and does not commit many serious sins; for he has nothing to goad and excite his soul. But if a man has devoted himself to the whole community and has been forced to endure the sins of all, and still remains firm and unwavering, piloting his soul through the tempest as in a calm, he is the one who deserves everyone's applause and admiration, for he has given proof enough of his own prowess.

So do not be surprised that I, who avoid the market-place and crowded society, have not many accusers. I should have no claim to admiration if I did not commit sin only because I was sleeping, or did not get a fall only because I was not wrestling, or was not wounded only because I was not fighting! Tell me, who can denounce and expose my depravity? This roof? This little cell? They cannot break into speech. Well then, the one who knows my character best of all, my mother? But in the first place, our lives are completely different; and we have never quarrelled. And even if this had happened, no mother is so heartless and such an enemy to her children that she would, without a compelling reason or someone's constraint, abuse and slander in front of everyone the son she had bred and borne and brought up. Yet if anyone were to examine my soul carefully, he would find that its weaknesses were many, as you yourself know quite well, though you are in the habit of praising me in public more highly than anyone else does.

To prove I am not saying this insincerely now, recollect how often I told you, on the many occasions when we discussed this question, that if anyone gave me the choice of where I should prefer to distinguish myself, in the government of the Church or in monastic life, I should go for the former every time. I never ceased commending to you those who were able to acquit themselves well in this ministry. And no one will deny that I should never have run away from what I used to commend if I had been competent to undertake it.

But what am I to do? Nothing is as useless for church government as this inactivity and detachment, which other people regard as a form of self-discipline, but which I have more as a veil for my own worthlessness, using it to cloak most of my failings and keep them from becoming obvious. When a man is used to enjoying so large a measure of freedom and living a life of complete leisure, however fine his nature may be, he is unsettled and confused by the want of discipline and loses a great deal of his natural ability through not exercising it. And when he is also a man of slow intellect and inexperienced in this kind of conflict, as I am, he will be no better than a waxwork, if he accepts this ministry.

This is why few of the men who come to these conflicts from that particular training-ground ever distinguish themselves. Most of them fail under test and endure bitter, hard troubles. And it is not surprising. For a contestant is no different from an untrained man, if his training and exercises have been for another sort of contest. Anyone who enters this arena should above all despise fame, should be superior to anger, and should be full of tact. But the devotee of the monastic life has no scope to exercise these qualities. He has but few to provoke him, so that he may practise restraining the force of his anger, or to admire and applaud him, so that he may be trained to scorn popular praises. And though in the churches there is a demand for tact, the monks think little of it. So when they enter these conflicts for which they have never practised, they are bewildered and dazed and grow helpless. They make no progress towards virtue, and in addition they often lose the good qualities they had when they started.

Basil: What! Are we to take men of the world, whose minds are set on mundane things, who are adepts at strife and abuse, who are full of all kinds of trickery and accustomed to a life of luxury, and set them over the government of the Church?

John: Hush, my friend! These men must not even be considered when our inquiry is for priests, but only those who mix and associate with all sorts of people and still manage to preserve more untarnished and steadfast than the monks themselves their purity and poise, their devoutness, patience, and frugality, and the other good qualities that belong to monks. For someone who has many faults, but can keep them out of view by living in isolation and disarm them by not associating with anybody, when he returns to social life, will achieve nothing except to become a laughing-stock, and will run worse risks than that. This very nearly happened to me, but that God's loving care quickly rescued me from that hazard.

This kind of man cannot pass unnoticed when he appears in public. All his faults are exposed, and as fire tests metals, so the touchstone of the ministry distinguishes men's souls. If a man is hot-tempered or petty or conceited or boastful or anything like that, it soon uncovers all his shortcomings and lays them bare. And not only does it lay them bare, it actually makes them more tough and intractable. For bodily wounds become harder to heal if they are chafed; and equally the diseases of the soul, if provoked and irritated, naturally grow more irksome and force their victims deeper into sin. They rouse a man, if he is not on his guard, to the love of popularity and to bragging and avarice; and they lead him on to luxury, self-indulgence, and indolence, and step by step to worse faults than these that are their natural offspring.

There are so many things in society which can enervate the soul and baulk its straight course. First of all, there is female company. For the president, being concerned with the whole flock, cannot simply take care of the part that consists of men and neglect the women, particularly as they require greater vigilance, since they easily slip into sin. On the contrary, the man appointed to exercise episcopal oversight must give as much thought, if not more, to the spiritual well-being of women. He must visit them in sickness, comfort them in sorrow, reprove them when indolent, and help them when overburdened. When this is done the Evil One will find many loopholes, unless he fortifies himself with a strict guard. A look strikes at his soul and unsettles it, and that from modest women, not only from the wanton. Flatteries unman him and courtesies enslave him, and fervent love, which is indeed the cause of all good things, becomes to those who misuse it the cause of incalculable evils.

It has sometimes happened, too, that continual cares have dulled the keenness of the intellect and made its wings heavier than lead; and anger has struck and smothered all within like a puff of smoke. Why mention the harm caused through grief, insults, abuse, and criticism from high and low, from wise and foolish? Persons of this last type, deprived as they are of right judgement, are the worst of cavillers, and will not readily accept explanations. But the wise prelate should not despise even these; he should rebut their accusations in public, very gently and humbly, being more prone to pardon their unreasonable complaints than to be indignant or angry.

For if St Paul was afraid he might incur the suspicion of theft among the disciples and so took others to help him in administering the money, "in order", he said, "that no man should blame us in the matter of this bounty which is ministered by us",[1] must not we do everything we can to destroy evil suspicions, however false they may be and however unreasonable and unlike the character we bear? We are not as far removed from any fault as Paul was from theft, and yet, far though he was from this evil practice, he did not disregard popular suspicion, although it was most un-reasonable and insane. For it certainly was insanity to form any such suspicion about that blessed and wonderful soul. But still, in spite of this, he sweeps away all possible grounds for suspicion, although it was so absurd and no one but a lunatic would have entertained it. He did not disregard people's mad suspicions. He did not say : "Who would ever think of suspecting me of any such thing, since everyone reveres and admires me, both for my miracles and for my

[1] 2 Cor. 8.20.

virtuous life?" No; quite the opposite—he foresaw and anti-
cipated this evil suspicion and tore it up by its root, or rather,
he did not let it grow at all. And why? "We take thought
for things honourable," he said, "not only in the sight of the
Lord, but also in the sight of men." [2] And we should show
just as much care as this, or even more, for preference. Then
we shall not only strangle evil reports at birth and eradicate
them, but even foresee their source far in advance, remove
the pretexts from which they spring, and not wait for them
to be established and bandied about on everyone's lips. By
that time it is no longer easy to extirpate them; indeed it is
very difficult and perhaps impossible. Nor is it done without damage, because it happens after popular suspicion has
done its worst.

But how long am I to continue chasing a will-o'-the-wisp?
Making a list of all the difficulties involved is like trying to
measure the ocean. For even if a man were absolutely free
from human passion—which is impossible—he must still put
up with untold troubles in order to correct the faults of
others. And when his own frailties are added, look at the
abyss of his toils and anxieties, and the host of sufferings
he must endure, if he would master his own sins and the sins
of others!

[2] 2 Cor. 8.21.

16

THE CONCLUSION OF JOHN'S APOLOGIA

BASIL: Do you mean that now, since you live by yourself, you have no need of toil, and no anxieties?

John: I have them even now. How could a human being, living this troublesome life, be free from anxieties and conflicts? But it is not at all the same thing to be plunged into the boundless ocean and to sail along a river. The difference between the two kinds of anxiety is as great as that. At present I should like to be helpful to others, if I could, and this is an object of much prayer to me. But if I cannot be of use to anyone else, I shall be satisfied if I am at least allowed to save my own soul and rescue it from the deep.

Basil: You seem to think that this is a great work. But do you suppose you will be saved at all, if you are never of any use to anyone else?

John: That was well and nobly spoken. I cannot myself believe it possible for anyone to be saved who never works for the salvation of his neighbour. It did not help that miserable man in the parable that he had not diminished his talent; it was his downfall that he had not increased it and restored it double. But still I think my punishment will be milder when I am called to account for not saving others than if it were for destroying the souls of others as well as my own, by becoming far worse in character after receiving so great an honour. At present I believe that my punishment will be just as much as the gravity of my sins requires; but after accepting this office I should receive, not twice or three times, but many times as much, for having made many others stumble and for accepting greater honour and then offending God who bestowed it on me.

This was the reason why he accused the Israelites more severely and showed that they deserved greater punishment, because they sinned after receiving the honours which he had bestowed on them. He said, "You only have I known of all the families of the earth : therefore I will visit upon you your iniquities"; [1] and again, "I took of your sons for prophets and of your young men for consecration".[2] And before the time of the prophets, when he wanted to show that sins received a much heavier penalty when they were committed by the priests than when they were committed by ordinary people, he commanded as great a sacrifice to be offered for the priests as for all the people.[3] This explicitly proves that the priest's wounds require greater help, indeed as much as those of all the people together. They would not have required greater help if they had not been more serious, and their seriousness is not increased by their own nature but by the extra weight of dignity belonging to the priest who dares to commit them.

But why speak of the men engaged in the ministry? Even the daughters of priests, who are of no significance for the priestly office, incur a far more severe penalty than others for the same sins, because of their fathers' dignity. The offence is the same (it is prostitution in both cases) when committed by them and the daughters of ordinary people, but their punishment is far greater.[4] You see how thoroughly God proves to you that he demands much more punishment of the ruler than of the subjects. He who for the sake of the priest punishes the priest's daughter more severely than others, obviously will not demand of the priest, to whom she

---

[1] Amos 3.2.   [2] Amos 2.11 (LXX).   [3] Lev. 4.3, 14.
[4] Lev. 21.9.

owes the increased penalty, just the same punishment as he demands of others, but one far more severe. That is only natural, for the damage does not devolve on him alone, but injures, too, the souls of his weaker brethren who look to him. This was what Ezekiel wanted to teach us, when he distinguished the judgement of the rams from that of the sheep.[5]

Do you think my fears are well-founded? On top of all I have said, if at present it costs me hard labour not to be completely mastered by my passions, at least I manage to put up with this labour and I do not run away from the conflict. Even now I am overtaken by vainglory, but I often recover. I see that I have been overcome, and sometimes I rebuke my soul for being enslaved. Vicious desires attack me even now, but the flame they light is less violent because my outward eyes cannot obtain fuel for the fire. But I am quite liberated from speaking evil of others or hearing evil spoken, since there is no one to talk with; to be sure, these walls cannot utter a sound! But it is not so easy to avoid anger, although there is nobody to provoke me. For often the memory of vicious men and what they have done comes upon me and makes my blood boil. But this does not last long, for I very soon restrain my temper and persuade it to calm down by saying that it is quite futile and utterly despicable to forget our own faults and meddle with those of our neighbours. But if I come among human society and am intercepted by innumerable distractions, I shall not be able to benefit from my own admonitions nor hit upon the thoughts that teach me sense. Men who are being driven over a precipice by a torrent or some other force, can foresee the destruction which finally awaits them, but cannot contrive any means to help themselves. So when I have tumbled into the

[5] Ezek. 34.17.

whirlpool of passions, I shall be able to see at a glance my punishment daily increasing; yet it will no longer be as easy for me as before to be master of myself, as I now am, and to rebuke all the raging fevers of my soul. For it is weak and puny, and falls an easy victim, not only to these passions, but to envy—the bitterest of all. It does not know how to bear insults and honours with moderation, but is inordinately exalted by the one and dejected by the other.

When savage beasts are vigorous and in good condition, they overcome all creatures that fight against them, especially those that are feeble and inexperienced in fighting; yet if you weaken them by starvation, you lull their spirits and quench most of their vigour, so that an animal of no great courage can undertake a tussle and can fight with them. So it is with the passions of the soul : if anyone weakens them, he makes them amenable to right reason; but if he fosters them carefully, he makes his struggle with them harder, and turns them into things so formidable that he lives the whole of his life in slavery and terror. And what is the food of these wild beasts? Of vainglory, it is honour and praise; of arrogance, excessive authority and power; of envy, the reputation of neighbours; of covetousness, the generosity of donors; of wantonness, luxury and the constant society of women; and other passions have other food. If I come into human society, all these passions will set upon me fiercely, tear my soul in pieces, terrify me and make my struggle with them harder. But if I stay here, they will be overcome, by the grace of God, and will be left with nothing but their snarl.

So I stick to this cell. I am isolated, unsociable, inhospitable. I put up with hearing a host of other complaints like these. I would gladly silence them, and feel pain and sorrow because I cannot. For it is not easy for me to become sociable and still remain secure as I am now. So, I beg you, pity but do not disparage the victim of such a perplexity.

Have I not yet persuaded you? Then the time has now come to let you into the one secret I have kept. Perhaps many people will find it hard to believe, but even so I shall not be ashamed to make it public. Although what I say is proof of an evil conscience and many sins, yet since God who is to be our judge knows everything perfectly, what advantage can I get from men's ignorance? And what is this secret? From the day on which you made me suspect what would happen my whole system has frequently been in danger of prostration—such was the terror and the bewilderment that gripped my spirit.

When I considered the glory of the Bride of Christ, her purity, her spiritual beauty, her wisdom, and her fair demeanour, and when I reckoned up my faults, I did not stop grieving for her and for myself, and in continual distress and perplexity I argued with myself like this:

"Who gave them this advice? Why did the Church of God make such a mistake? How did she so provoke her Master as to be handed over to me, the most worthless of men, and to endure such terrible disgrace?"

As I turned this over in my mind again and again and could not bear the very thought of so horrible a thing, I lay mute, like an epileptic, unable to see or hear. When this condition of utter helplessness left me (for at times it would abate), it was succeeded by tears and bewilderment. And after I had wept my fill, the terror returned again instead, agitating and deranging and convulsing my mind. That is the sort of distraction I have been living in recently, and you did not know, and thought I was spending my time in perfect calm. But now I will try to disclose to you the tempest of my soul. Perhaps when you hear it you will forgive me and forget my misdeeds. But how, oh how shall I disclose it? If you wanted to see it truly, you could only do so by laying bare my heart. Since that cannot be done, I will try to show you by some faint image, as far as I can, the fog of bewilderment I am in; and you must try to infer my bewilderment from this image.

Suppose the daughter of the king who rules the whole earth beneath the sun is betrothed to someone. Suppose this girl is so wonderfully beautiful as to surpass all humanity, and in this excels by far the whole of womankind; and she has so virtuous a character that she leaves far behind all men who have ever been or ever shall be; and the charm of her disposition goes beyond all ideals of philosophy, as the loveliness of her face eclipses all bodily beauty. Her suitor is enamoured of the girl for these reasons and, quite apart from them, is deeply in love with her, too, and by his passion puts into the shade the most ardent lovers that ever were. Then while he is on fire with the spell she casts, he is told by someone that the wonderful girl he loves is about to be married to some vile outcast of mongrel birth, crippled in body and in every way utterly worthless. Have I brought before your mind some faint idea of my grief? Will it do if I end my simile at this point? It is enough, I think, to describe my bewilderment, and that was the only point of the comparison. But to show you the extent of my terror and dismay, let me go on now with another illustration.

Imagine an army composed of infantry, cavalry, and marines. Let the muster of its triremes blot out the sea, while the regiments of its infantry and cavalry smother the broad plains and the very heights of the mountains. Let the bronze of its armour flash back at the sun, and the glitter of the helmets and shields mirror the rays that stream down. Let the clash of spears and the neighing of horses reach the very sky, and let neither sea nor land be visible, but everywhere bronze and steel. Against all this let the enemy be arrayed, a wild and barbarous horde. And let the hour of conflict be at hand.

Suppose someone suddenly seizes a raw lad, brought up in the fields, knowing nothing except the use of the shepherd's pipe and crook. He invests him in brazen mail, leads him round the whole camp, and shows him companies and captains, archers, slingers, officers, generals, infantry, cavalry, spearmen, ships and their captains, the soldiers crowded on the ships, and the multitude of engines of war ready on board. He points out, too, the enemy's full array, their menacing faces, their strange type of weapons, and their vast numbers, and the ravines, sheer cliffs, and mountain tracks. He points out also on the enemy's side horses flying by magic, armed soldiers borne through the air, and witchcraft of every power and form. He describes all the disasters of war, too : the cloud of spears, the showers of arrows, the great mist and darkness, the pitch-black night caused by the multitude of missiles blotting out the sun's rays by their sheer density, the dust blinding the eyes no less than this darkness, the torrents of blood, the groans of those who fall, the battle-cries of those who stand, the heaps of slain, chariot wheels dripping with blood, horses and riders thrown headlong by the multitude of dead bodies, the ground nothing but a sludge of blood and arrows and javelins, horses' hoofs and human heads lying in heaps, a man's arm and a chariot wheel, a helmet and a transfixed chest, swords spattered with human brains, and the broken head of an arrow with an eye spitted upon it.

Let him describe, too, all the perils of the fleet : some ships ablaze in mid-sea, others foundering with the soldiers on board, the roar of the waves, the cries of the sailors, the shouts of the soldiers, the sea-foam mixed with blood and dashing over all the ships alike, corpses on the deck, others sinking, others floating, others washed ashore, and others in the water washed about by the waves and clogging the passage of the ships. And when he has pointed out in detail all the tragedies of war, let him go on to describe the horrors of captivity and slavery which is worse than any kind of death. And when he has said all, let him give the lad the order to mount horse at once and take command of all that host. Do you think that raw youth will be adequate for that command? Do you not think he will faint at the first glance?

Do not imagine I am exaggerating or think that because we are shut up in this body like a prison and can see nothing of the invisible world, what I say is overstated. You would have seen a much vaster and much more terrifying conflict than this, if you had been able to see with these material eyes the devil's crepuscular battle-line and its furious onset. It has no bronze or steel, no horses or chariots or chariot-wheels, no flames or missiles. It has none of this visible equipment, but other engines of war far more terrifying than these. Enemies of this sort have no need of breastplate or shield, sword or spear. No, but the very sight of that accursed host is enough to make a man's heart fail him, unless it is mighty stout and has the benefit of God's special providence, even more than its own courage.

If it were possible to strip off this body, or even to keep it on and see clearly and undismayed with the naked eye the devil's whole battle-line and the warfare he wages against us, you would see no torrents of blood, no dead bodies, but so many spiritual corpses and such horrible wounds that you would think all that picture of warfare which I have just described to you was mere child's play, and sport rather than war, so many there are every day who perish. The two kinds of wounds do not produce the same necrosis; the difference between the two corresponds with the difference between soul and body. When the soul receives a blow and falls, it does not lie insensible, like the body, but is immediately tormented by the ravaging of an evil conscience, and after its release from this world it is given over to eternal punishment at the hour of judgement. And if anyone feels no pain at the devil's blows, his danger is increased by this lack of sensation. For the man who does not smart at the first blow will soon receive a second, and after that a third. Whenever the Evil One finds a soul supine and indifferent to his previous attacks, he never stops striking until that man breathes his last.

If you care to investigate his method of attack, you will find it is far more severe and varied than it seems. No one else knows as many variations of trickery and guile as that Evil One. This is how he has gained his great power. No one can feel such implacable hatred for his worst enemies as the Evil One feels for the human race. And if you investigate the eagerness with which he fights, here too it would be simply ridiculous to compare human beings with him. If you picked out the most ferocious and savage beasts and compared them with the devil's frenzy, you would find them gentle and tame by comparison, such a fury does he breathe out when he attacks our souls. Then again, the duration of a battle is short and even in that short period there are many respites; the approach of night, weariness of slaughter, time taken for food, and many other things naturally bring the soldier to a standstill, and so he is able to strip off his armour, enjoy a brief respite, refresh himself with food and drink, and revive his former strength in various other ways. But when facing the Evil One you must never lay down your arms; you must never take any sleep if you want to remain for ever unhurt. You must do one of two things : either take off your armour and so fall and perish, or stand always armed and watchful. For he always stands with his forces marshalled, waiting for our moments of inadvertence, and he takes more trouble to damn our souls than we take to save them. The fact that he is unseen by us and that his attacks are very sudden (which is the chief cause of untold evils to those who are not continually on guard) proves that this kind of warfare is far more difficult than the other.

Did you, then, want me to lead Christ's soldiers? Truly that would have been to act as the devil's general; for when the man who ought to marshal and dispose the rest is himself the most inexperienced and the weakest of all, he betrays by his inexperience the men put under his charge and so acts the devil's general, not Christ's.

But why are you sighing and weeping? For my present position does not deserve commiseration, but gladness and joy.

Basil: But not mine ! My position deserves infinite regrets. Even now I can hardly grasp just how deep in misfortune you have brought me. I came to you with the object of discovering what excuse I should make on your behalf to those who were accusing you. But instead you are sending me away loaded with one care on top of another. I am not concerned now with the excuse I shall make to them for you, but with the excuse I shall make to God for myself and my own sins. I beg and implore your help, if you care for me at all, "if there is any comfort in Christ, if any consolation of love, if any tender mercies and compassions".[6] For you know that it was you yourself more than anyone who brought me into this danger. Give me a helping hand. Say or do something to restore me, and do not let yourself leave

[6] Phil. 2.1.

me alone for a moment, but now more than ever before share your life with me.

I smiled and said : "What can I offer? How can I help you to carry so heavy a burden? And yet, since such is your desire, take courage, my dear friend, for whenever it proves possible for you to have a respite from the cares of your office, I will come to your side and encourage you, and nothing shall be left undone that lies within my power."

At this he wept even more, and rose to go. Then I clasped him and kissed his head, and led him out, urging him to bear his fortune bravely. "For I trust in Christ," I said, "who called you and set you over his own sheep, that you will gain such assurance from this ministry that when I stand in peril on that great Day, you will receive me into your everlasting habitation."